FRANCIS BRENNAN'S
BOOK *of* HOUSEHOLD
MANAGEMENT

Gill Books

Hume Avenue

Park West

Dublin 12

www.gillbooks.ie

Gill Books is an imprint of M.H. Gill and Co.

978 07171 7552 9

Designed by www.grahamthew.com

Edited by Alison Walsh

Printed by T J International, Cornwall

This book is typeset in 11 on 15.5pt Hoefler Titling .

The paper used in this book comes from the wood pulp of managed forests. For every tree felled, at least one tree is planted, thereby renewing natural resources.

A CIP catalogue record for this book is available from the British Library.

FRANCIS BRENNAN'S BOOK *of* HOUSEHOLD MANAGEMENT

How to Create a Happy Home

⬦⬦⬦⬦⬦⬦⬦⬦⬦⬦⬦⬦⬦⬦⬦⬦⬦⬦⬦⬦⬦⬦⬦⬦⬦⬦⬦

Francis Brennan

GILL BOOKS

FRANCIS BRENNAN is a national treasure and the bestselling author of *It's the Little Things* and *Counting My Blessings*. He fronts one of Ireland's most popular TV shows, *At Your Service*, where his wit and charm have endeared him to a mass of fans across the country, as well as *Francis Brennan's Grand Tour*. Together with his brother John he is co-owner of the five-star Park Hotel Kenmare.

Contents

Introduction

Chapter One

A Little Bit of Sparkle – Getting the Basics Right

Your Household Planner ... 10

Low-Impact Cleaning ... 15

Windows and Mirrors ... 23

Kitchen Cleanliness ... 24

The Spring Clean ... 30

Keeping a Pet-Friendly Home Clean ... 34

Cleaning Your Car ... 39

Chapter Two

Tidiness is Next to Godliness

Clutter ... 48

Disposing, Donating and Recycling ... 52

Storage Solutions ... 54

The Art of Folding ... 61

Paper Trail ... 63

Toy Storage ... 65

Photo Storage and Printing ... 68

Chapter Three

Your Cosy Home – Furniture, Interior and Other Lovely Things

Finding Space ... 75

Sofas and Covers ... 78

Cushions and Throws ... 81

Curtains and Blinds ... 85

Paints and Wallpaper ... 87

Floors ... 94

Wood and Linoleum ... 97

Green Shoots ... 98

The Kitchen Garden ... 100

Chapter Four

The Littlest Room in the House

The Tub ... 113

Bathroom Surfaces... 115

It Has to Be Done ... 116

Bathroom Bliss ... 118

Soap and Salts ... 120

Chapter Five

The Linen Cupboard

Before Washing ... 127

Easy Patching... 131

The Washing Machine ... 131

Stain Removal ... 133

Sorting Laundry ... 136

Washing Tips ... 138

Matching Pairs ... 139

Drying ... 141

The Linen Cupboard... 143

Ironing ... 146

Chapter Six

Waste Not, Want Not

Food Waste ... 154

The Bin ... 160

Composting ... 163

Household Budgets ... 165

Wasting Money ... 166

Repairs ... 170

Upcycling ... 173

Chapter Seven

Your Almanac of Household Essentials

Home-made Cleaners ... 180

Some Simple Home Hacks ... 183

Keeping Your Home Safe ... 188

Epilogue

INTRODUCTION

When I was a young boy, my mother used to do a spring clean. Do you remember that? The parish priest or some important person would announce that he or she was going to pay a visit and Mum would get started with her cleaning list. After a winter with all of us huddled up inside, and coal fires burning in the grate, the house would have a lovely layer of soot and dust that needed special cleaning. Now, before my mother kills me, the house was never *dirty* – but it was considered a necessity in those days, to do a once-a-year, really deep clean: rugs would be lifted and taken outdoors to air, and then to have the dust beaten out of them, curtains would be taken down, nets whitened, tablecloths laundered, windows cleaned, and Dad would be sent to clean the gutters. I can't say I that I ever saw the parish priest examining them for signs of dirt, but the point was, the spring clean was part of the yearly ritual of making a home sparkle.

There were weekly and monthly rituals too. I remember the Monday wash, the Friday cleaning of the cooker and so on. Housework in those days was a full-time job, with the wash beginning on Mondays, swishing around in a big tub, before being rinsed and put through the mangle – remember the mangle?! – then hung out to dry in the Irish wind and rain. And, if Mum was ever lucky enough to get a few good drying days, the wash would come back in, be put in the hot press to air, then ironed, then put away in drawers and wardrobes, before the whole cycle would begin again. I'm amazed at how Mum ever managed, running a house with five children in it and a husband who worked 12-hour days. But manage she did, and beautifully.

I'm tempted to think that it must have been much harder for her in 'the olden days', but I have since come to rethink that notion. Of course, housework would have been more labour intensive then, with no dishwasher or dryer – unless you count us Brennans, the human dishwashers! – no online grocery ordering, no convenience food; but there would have been that all-important commodity: time. Life wasn't a constant round of activity, the way it is nowadays, with mums and dads both working, kids out at school or at soccer matches, scouts, music lessons and all that kind of thing. Time nowadays is at a premium, and no person wants to spend his or her precious free time hoovering the skirting boards.

Which is where *Mr Brennan's Guide to Household Management* comes in. I'm sure there will be those among you who will wonder what I have to say about housework – sure, you must hardly live at home, Francis, I can hear you say. And those of you who will have seen me wrestling to put on a duvet cover on live television might be a bit sceptical of my knowledge in that department, but running a hotel teaches you a lot about the importance and the pleasures of a tidy, clean place – how warm and welcoming it can feel, how much pleasure it can give you and others. My hotel is my 'home', and when I welcome people into it, I want them to feel that they can truly relax, knowing that the silver is polished, the napkins are laundered, the sofas cosy and clean.

Some of the old ways are still useful even today and we shouldn't throw them away, from household budgets to working with the seasons and from traditional home cleaners that are well worth using to clever shopping, but I know that we have to be sensible about how that all fits into our busy modern lives. There's a lot to learn from newer concepts like recycling (I hope you all recycle!) and upcycling, which means finding a new purpose for old things, rather than throwing them out, as well as using modern technology to make our lives that much easier. I also think that I know a thing or two about modern family homes, thanks to my friend, Cathy. I often pop in to see her in Dublin and I see how she manages a busy home and family, working as a team with her husband and children and taking it all in her stride. In fact, I asked Cathy for some tips, which you'll see sprinkled throughout the text.

Modern life isn't easy, but with a little bit of help, you can get your own 'hotel' spick and span, with the minimum of fuss, so that you have more time for the nice things in life, like relaxation, friends and family.

Good luck and happy homemaking!

CHAPTER ONE

A Little Bit of Sparkle – Getting the Basics Right

"Housework won't kill you, but then again, why take the chance?"

PHYLLIS DILLER

A 2017 *Good Housekeeping* article compiled a list of the kind of chores we 'should' all be doing to have nice, clean homes, and it caused a bit of a stir. As one commentator remarked, 'Well. You know. It's a nice idea. I really, really want to be this person. Unfortunately, this person and I have never met.' I was tickled pink!

However, what I took from the article was not that housekeeping should be a stick to beat ourselves with – there are quite enough of those – but that it might be helpful to put some planning into the whole business, and to do some sharing-out of household tasks. If there's one thing I've learned from watching Cathy, it's that housekeeping nowadays isn't, God help us, a woman's work, as it would have been in my own mother's day: it's a team effort. And working with a team takes a bit of thought and cooperation.

To show you just how much things have changed, here's a schedule from a 'housewife' in 1921, quoted in a magazine article of the time. This lady was the mother of five children:

6:00 am – Get up and heat the milk for the baby, at the same time taking cereal from fireless cooker and putting it on stove to heat for breakfast.

6:15 – Feed baby, dress myself and second child. Oversee older children as they dress.

7:15 – As table was set the night before, I have only to put on the cream, milk, butter, bread for the electric toaster, start coffee, and serve cereal.

7:30 – Breakfast. We always have eggs in some form, which are quick to prepare – shirred eggs or omelet can be left in a slow oven while the cereal is being eaten. The two older children always help put the dishes on the table and clear it off for me.

8:15 – I wash the dishes, scalding them in the drainer so that they dry quickly, the children helping me wipe them and put them away.

9:00 – With the children's help I make the beds, wipe up the floors of the bedrooms with a dust mop, and also dust the furniture that needs it.

9:30 – Bathe the baby and set bathroom in order.

10:00 – Feed the baby and put her in her pen on the porch.

10:15 – Rinse out diapers for the day, and dust and put in order sitting-room and dining-room.

11:00 – Prepare dinner after putting baby in crib for long nap.

12:15 – Dinner

1:00 PM – Wash dishes with children's help as before – the oldest puts the second child in bed for a short nap. When dishes are out of the way, I sweep the kitchen floor and back porch. As we live on our front porch in summer, I alternate the care of the porch with the living room, as there is not time to do both on the same day.

2:00 – Feed baby and put her back in the pen again.

2:15 – Take twenty minutes for nap and then dress for afternoon.

3:00 – Dress the second child for the afternoon. Take mending or sewing on the porch with the children.

5:00 – Start supper.

5:30 – Give the two babies their supper and put them to bed.

6:15–6:30 – Supper when their father comes home.

7:15 – Wash dishes and set table for breakfast with father's and children's help.

8:00 – Older children go to bed.

Can you believe it? I was very impressed by the big breakfast, which I think is a great idea. Nowadays, so many of us skip this vital meal. And, when I think of it, my own mother's day wouldn't have been very different. My father worked all God's hours in his shop in Stepaside, so she had a strict routine to keep the house going and to keep us all in check. A lot of what Mum did at home came from her own upbringing on a farm in Sligo, which was kept beautifully, neatly whitewashed with a lovely garden.

The point is, I don't think any of us today would recognise this woman; even mums or dads who don't work outside the home spend their days in a dizzying whirl of homework, soccer practice and everything else that goes on in a busy family. Modern life has certainly changed, and the way we clean our homes has too.

What I've learned from my own experience is that 'little and often' is key. It might surprise some of you, but I do half an hour of cleaning every day. Really! The reason I do this is because I find that just doing a little bit regularly is much easier than being faced with a Herculean task once a month. Have you ever forgotten to put on a wash, or to empty the dishwasher? Before you know it, the laundry basket is overflowing and the sink full of plates and cups. I know that 'little and often' might seem obvious, but it really helps with a sense of feeling in control of things.

I do my clean in the mornings, and when I come home after a long day at the hotel I'm delighted to sit on the couch and relax, rather than look at the mess. My daily jobs include: emptying the dishwasher, making the bed, putting newspapers and recycling into the bin, giving the place a quick flick with a duster and a bit of general tidying. To this I add – every couple of days – a run-around with the vacuum cleaner. Weekly, I clean the bathroom and kitchen surfaces and file any post that I've received, so that I don't end up with a big pile of it on the hall table. Hey presto, the basics are taken care of. The big stuff, like fridge and oven cleaning, which makes my heart sink, if I'm completely honest, I do once a month, and other tasks, like defrosting the freezer or tidying up my cluttered larder, are every-two-months jobs at best.

The point is, a little planning or scheduling really helps me to remember what I have to do and when – and saves on that awful panic when you know you have guests arriving and the place looks as if a bomb hit it! It's enough to be preparing for your dinner party or lunch without adding having to spend three hours hoovering and dusting into the bargain. And, I don't know about you, but I am terrible for putting things off, so, if I have something in my weekly schedule, I feel that I have to do it, whether I like it or not.

The daily tasks are easy enough to remember, but I found myself downloading a helpful housekeeping schedule from the internet – you can even get an app that will help you! Schedules are helpful if you share a house, or, as my friend Cathy has found, in divvying up the tasks among the children. It's much easier to give children a clear list of daily chores and expect them to do them than it is to nag them every single day to do something that you've just decided needs doing. If Mary knows that she has to tidy her bedroom on a Wednesday, she'll do that and know that it's expected of her – but if you suddenly ask her when she's in the middle of some game, there'll be a row. With planning, everyone knows where he or she stands – remember, a planner is not an invitation to do everything yourself!

Planning also helps you to remember those essential jobs like checking your carbon monoxide or smoke alarm, that kind of thing. But be kind to yourself: say you are out all day on a Monday, then at an aerobics class, don't schedule in a big bit of housework for when you come home exhausted! Make Monday the day for the bare minimum and do a little bit more on the days that you are freer.

And remember, whatever kind of planning you decide to do, I would try not to get bogged down in a hundred 'to-do lists', as they can be totally overwhelming. You look at the list and find that you haven't ticked off one or two items and it's a disaster! Give yourself a break – nobody died, as my mother used to say. Look on your schedule as a flexible thing that will adapt to surprises and upsets. For example, my friend Cathy is a busy working mum; she was planning to go away for a week and spent the previous week making freezer meals for her teenaged children, putting them into the freezer, neatly labelled, feeling that she was a great mum altogether. Of course, while she was away they completely ignored them – instead, they used the 'emergency money' she left out to order in pizza every night! The point I'm making is that life won't always go according to plan, so, be flexible.

YOUR HOUSEHOLD PLANNER

Here are a few examples of what could go into a planner.

DAILY

- Put dishes into dishwasher/wash up.

- Tidy away newspapers and magazines.

- Make the beds.

- Open the post and check what needs to be done that day and what can wait.

- Wipe the countertops and cooker – just a quick wipe with a damp cloth.

- Put dirty clothes in the laundry basket.

- Make lunches – get your children to do this as soon as they are able, and to put their lunchboxes in the dishwasher when they come home from school.

- Sweep the kitchen floor.

- Sit down for 20 minutes and have a cup of tea and a read of a magazine or book. This might seem a bit odd to add to a planner, but sometimes we need to remember to make time for ourselves. So, now you have it scheduled in and you are more likely to do it.

WEEKLY

My mother would have had a strict weekly routine. Monday was always wash day, just as it was for everyone else at the time. The only occasion I can ever remember my mother doing the washing on a Sunday was the time she had a row with Dad and refused to come into the living room and watch the Sunday movie with the rest of us. To this day, I have no idea what the row was about, but it shocked us all, because it was the one and only row they ever had!

So, if Monday was wash day, Tuesday was for the ironing (if she was lucky enough to have dry clothes), Wednesday was for the garden, Thursday for shopping, Friday was for tidying our school clothes and sorting out our weekend routine. On Saturday she'd take us swimming in Tara Street Baths, or she'd take the girls, Susan and Kate, to hockey matches. Dad was out of the picture, as were so many dads in those days: he left for the shop at 8.30, returned home at five to one, had lunch, slept for 10 minutes *only*, then he'd be off back to work until 9 o'clock at night, when supper would be kept for him. Of course, your weekly planner will look a bit different! Here are a few things you might include:

- Cook a home-cooked Sunday dinner and get all of the family around the table. Another surprise in a planner, but with family time at a premium, maybe it's worth reminding yourself and everyone else to get together once a week. Even better, schedule in your teenager or your older child to cook a meal; it may not be 'haute cuisine', but it will broaden their repertoire – start them with simple things like chicken fajitas, which are easy-peasy, and then suggest that they try spaghetti bolognese, meatballs etc. A friend of mine left her 18-year-old home alone when she went away for a weekend, and he cooked himself a lamb stew following the instructions on the diced lamb packet – so they might surprise you!

- Select and allocate daily chores: making the beds, tidying bedrooms, putting yesterday's newspaper into the recycling, filling and emptying the dishwasher, walking and feeding the dog.

- Hoover. How often you do this depends on a lot of things. If you're out at work all day, you won't need to hoover more than once or twice a week; if you're at home, or if you have pets, you might well find that hoovering is a daily task – or certainly in busy areas, like the kitchen and living room.

- Clean the bathroom.

- Compile the weekly shopping list – checking cupboards, fridge and freezer to see what you have first.

- Do the weekly shop – I'll talk more about how to streamline this later on in the book. It's the one thing many of us find to be a chore – quite literally.

- Mop kitchen and bathroom floors.

- Do the recycling/put out the bin.

- File correspondence. I used to do this every few months and found that I had to spend a whole afternoon at a job I hated, so now I do it once a week.

- Call a friend/send a birthday card/buy a present. Again, it might seem like nonsense to schedule in a phone call, but we know how busy we all get nowadays. I certainly find a reminder to call someone helpful, and the same is true for reminders for birthdays, Mother's Day and other occasions. I put everything in my smartphone calendar and it reminds me by buzzing all the time – annoying, but I don't forget the important things!

- Water and feed plants, lift weeds and do a little tidy in the garden.

- Wash bedlinen and towels – weekly is a bit of a big 'ask' for this, so I always try to change the sheets and wash towels fortnightly.

MONTHLY

I don't know about you, but these are the tasks that I find harder to achieve. I'm fine with my daily tidy, even my weekly cleaning of the bathroom, but the monthly tasks I'm inclined to put off. Who really wants to clean their oven every month?! However, I find that if I get even the fridge and cooker cleaned, and do a bit of dusting, I'm delighted with myself. And following my daily and weekly schedule pattern, I try to fit in something nice too, like a lunch with friends, to reward myself for all of that hard work. Monthly 'to dos' could include the following:

- Descale the coffee pot/kettle.

- Clean the fridge and remove any jars that are no longer used.

- Wipe grease off the cooker hood.

- Clean the oven and microwave.

- Run the washing machine/dishwasher on empty to clean them.

- Hoover under the sofa, along the skirting boards and in dusty corners.

- Tidy out your sock drawer – I have a lovely system for folding socks and other small items, but if I don't stay on top of it, it all turns into a big mess!

- De-mould the bathroom ceiling/tiles; if you wipe your tiles down every day after you shower, this task will be much easier.

- Tidy rubbish out of the car and check the tyres to see that they are properly inflated.

EVERY THREE MONTHS

- Tidy your wardrobe. You don't have to pull everything out, but if your clothes filing system has gone a bit awry, put everything back in place; put to one side things that you haven't worn in the last three months (seasonal items notwithstanding).

- Defrost the freezer.

- Wash the windows – some people put this into the monthly list, which is fair enough, particularly if we've had a lot of rain, but I believe in aiming for reality, not fantasy!

- Airing is a job that should be done regularly, but every three months, throw open the windows and doors and let the air circulate. Obviously, pick a nice day to do this!

- If you have 'nice things', now is the time to give them a good clean or polish: my mother used to set us to polishing the silver every three months – it was a task I didn't relish, but I loved the shining silver afterwards.

- Air duvets and pillows – I wash pillows every three months or so, but in rotation, so I don't have every pillow in the house wet at the same time.

- Check the oil in your car.

ANNUAL AND BI-ANNUAL JOBS

- Service your boiler and car – anything that has a motor needs at least an annual check.

- Wash paintwork and skirting boards.

- Swap lightweight clothes for winter ones and vice versa. Store clothes away.

- Get your winter or summer duvet laundered, depending on the season.

- Reorganise your linen cupboard and larder.

- Steam clean carpets and upholstery.

- Check gutters for any blocks, such as leaves/moss.

This schedule is just an outline of things you might like to remember. That doesn't mean that you're a failure if you don't. We are all so busy nowadays that perfection on the household front is not always attainable. Also, cleaning ladies are only for those who can afford them, but you could ask people to give you a voucher for a cleaning service as a present – and use it to hire someone to give the house a really deep clean. Maybe your mother-in-law might give you one!

Don't forget, while most of us can stay on top of the daily chores, it's the bigger jobs that are more difficult nowadays, so ...

- Share the jobs out.

- Get some help – you might be surprised to find that friends and family will help you with tasks that are getting you down, like decluttering or spring cleaning – they often prefer this to doing their own jobs at home!

- Save for a once-off clean to get things under control or ask for a voucher for a cleaner as a present.

- Schedule in the things you like to do as well as the things you have to do.

- Reward yourself for jobs well done!

CATHY'S TIP:

Unpopular jobs cause rows between the children, so make sure to share them out and follow a strict rota, so there'll be no fighting.

LOW-IMPACT CLEANING

Once you've decided on your schedule, you'll be feeling very pleased with yourself, I'm sure, but have you given any thought to what you're going to use to clean your home? I used to be a great man for whatever was easy and quick – wipes and sprays, mould removers, special dusting cloths – all that kind of thing. Now, though, I've come to understand that things like lemon juice and vinegar and that old favourite, bread soda, will do just as good a job; and they won't fill your home with noxious fumes – at least, if you are careful. I'll be going into detail about all of these as we go along in the book, but to start, here are a few of my favourite cleaning products and where you can use them. Just a note, though – don't be tempted to take shortcuts with food preparation surfaces – clean them with a suitable cleaner, and do so often, to avoid any chance of germs. Also, if you live with youngsters, old people or anyone who is ill, you may need to take extra care with cleaning.

Lemon juice – is one of those wonder things, with so many uses, from making a soothing drink with honey for sore throats, or a pick-me-up breakfast drink with hot water, but it's also brilliant around the house. You can use lemons to clean ovens and microwaves, to remove limescale and (mixed with salt) to clean old pots and remove rust stains. Some recipes even use one part lemon juice to two parts olive oil as a home-made furniture polish! It's also a brilliant odour remover. See my Almanac, in Chapter 7, for more lemon recipes. You need to avoid using lemons on porous surfaces, though, and on surfaces that don't like acid.

Bicarbonate of soda – mixed with bleach, it is brilliant at cleaning grubby tile grout, as well as by itself for cleaning bathroom surfaces, fridges, ovens and stainless steel. It can also absorb nasty smells if you leave a cupful in a bowl in the fridge – it's fantastic! It's also called baking soda, of course, and when I was looking things up about this wonder substance, I was reminded of something funny that happened in the hotel. We always have lovely Christmas services in Kenmare – in both the Catholic and the Protestant churches, with carols and candlelight and that sort of thing – it really is magical. After the services, we have people back for hot drinks and mince pies. The chefs always make them first and leave them out before they go home, ready to be served, with lots of whipped cream and icing sugar. Delicious, I'm sure you'll agree. On this particular Christmas Eve, the chef left out a bowl of 'icing sugar' which we all liberally sprinkled on our mince pies. I bit into mine and had the funniest burning sensation on my lips. I looked around the room and there were puckered lips everywhere! Only later did I realise that the icing sugar was baking soda!

Vinegar – no, not your best aged balsamic, but plain old spirit vinegar – excellent for cleaning mirrors and windows and shining taps, as well as cleaning the loo, even removing stains. Another wonder cleaner which I'll talk about later. And see my Almanac for some sweet-smelling vinegar cleaners! Both bicarb and vinegar can be bought in large quanitites for home use in DIY stores, as can liquid bicarb – to save you the bother of mixing.

Citric acid – can be bought in packs at the hardware store and will remove limescale from appliances like dishwashers, washing machines and kettles. Check to ensure that your item is made from stainless steel.

Toothpaste – I know, toothpaste might seem a little 'out there' but it can be just the ticket for removing certain stains. *Reader's Digest* has found no fewer than 16 ways of using good old toothpaste for everything from buffing up grubby shoes and trainers to removing stains from your iron, getting rid of ink stains on clothes, cleaning babies' bottles (add a little dab to your scrubbing brush to get rid of that sour milk smell), defogging glass and swimming goggles (you apply a thin layer and then wipe off) – even cleaning piano keys! Make sure you use the old-fashioned white toothpaste, though – no blue gels or whitening toothpastes.

Borax – an old-fashioned sink and drain unblocker and also a good stain remover in the washing machine. Borax itself is no longer available as a cleaning product, but look out for 'borax substitute' in your hardware store, which gives the same cleaning results.

Methylated spirits – my granny used to use methylated spirits on bee and wasp stings, believe it or not, but I wouldn't recommend it. This purple spirit is good for removing things like candle-wax stains from your favourite coffee table, as a paint thinner and for cleaning metal.

Washing-up liquid – this might not seem to fit into the category of 'low-impact', but washing-up liquid isn't nearly as harsh as other modern cleaners, and you can use it everywhere. A tiny drop added to a spray bottle with vinegar provides you with an instant bathroom cleaner, for example. I've devoted a whole space to the wonders of washing-up liquid below. I was amused to read that one lady used it to clean her horse's tail – it's cheaper than horse shampoo and just as good, she says! Horse lovers among you can let me know if this is true.

Salt – such a simple thing with so many uses. Salt can be used to remove red wine stains from carpets and upholstery, as well as things that might leak in your oven or onto your lovely hob. Soak the spillage in salt and then wipe it away. Salt is also a brilliant cleaner of metals like copper. If you have copper pots and pans, you can make a paste with salt, lemon juice and a dash of vinegar. Rub it on and your copper will shine once more. Salt is also a brilliant de-stinker of smelly shoes! Sprinkle some into your pongy trainers, leave and then hoover up.

Be careful not to mix some of these things together: it's no accident that children use vinegar and bread soda in those home-made 'volcano' kits – the results of mixing the two are spectacular. You have been warned! Other things not to mix together are:

- **Hydrogen peroxide and vinegar.**
- **Bleach and vinegar.**
- **Bleach and ammonia.**

Bleach can be mixed with bread soda, but nothing else.

Speaking of ammonia, I remember that you used to be able to get it in a ceramic bottle with a ridged surface to it, presumably to help with grip, but it has a truly awful smell. The mention of ammonia reminded me of this young fellow who worked at the hotel long ago. His dad asked him to clean the car. 'Use vinegar!' he roared at him, because in those days the seats weren't fabric, of course. So, the young fellow set to, wiping every single surface in the car with the contents of the vinegar bottle he'd brought out with him. He was only delighted with his work. The next day, the family were about to set off in the car to Mass and the young fellow's father opened the car door – to be met with the overwhelming smell of ammonia! He nearly killed his son!

HOW TO ... USE WASHING-UP LIQUID

As a stain remover. It's gentler than washing powder, and a little squirt – neat – onto stains, particularly grease stains, will work wonders.

For patio furniture. A squirt of washing-up liquid into a bucket of warm water and you have a mild cleaner for your patio table and chairs. You can also attack the grill part of your barbie with diluted washing-up liquid. Spray on, allow to soak in, then scrub away the grime!

As an all-purpose cleaner, diluted in a little warm water. You can use it on practically every surface, so it's great if you've run out of your favourite spray.

As a general degreaser on your cooker hood, kitchen cabinets and splashback. Just a little squirt into warm water and you have an instant cleaning solution.

As an inexpensive cleaner for porous surfaces like marble.

As a carpet stain remover. Washing-up liquid can be as effective as specialist cleaners on a number of stains.

To wash delicates. In a pinch – a dessert spoon into a basin of water will do the job if you've run out of mild clothes cleaner. Don't try this on fabrics that say 'dry clean only' though.

As a hairbrush cleaner. A squirt in a bowl of hot water, pop the hairbrushes in and leave to soak. Rinse and leave to dry – hey presto: clean hairbrushes!

As a home-made ant and flea killer. You mix one teaspoon of washing-up liquid with warm water in a spray bottle and spray the critters. I think that ant powder is easier, as you can simply vacuum it up, but washing-up liquid will do in an ant crisis!

To remove pests from plants. Spray a diluted solution of washing-up liquid onto your plant's leaves and wipe pests away.

Don't use washing-up liquid in your washing machine or dishwasher if you have run out of tablets or powder – it will make far too many big soapy bubbles.

Of course, with all the chat about home-made volcanoes, I've probably given you the fright of your life about using home-made products. What can you use safely and where?

Stainless steel – a little diluted washing-up liquid is just the thing for daily cleaning; for tougher stains on stainless steel, it's time to get out the bread soda: a tablespoon mixed with a little water, spread liberally over the stain and then wiped away after 20 minutes will do the job.

A mix of vinegar and lemon juice in your spray bottle, wiped clean with a dry cloth, will keep your stainless steel shiny. A mixture of lemon juice and salt is abrasive enough to remove pesky rust stains, but be careful when you scrub not to damage the stainless steel – a nice circular motion should be just the ticket.

Marble – not many of us have marble tabletops, kitchen surfaces or bathrooms any more, because newer surfaces are that much easier to look after, particularly if you have children, but if you do have marble, be gentle with it and use a mild cleaner with no bleach in it. Acid is the enemy of marble, so avoid it. That means no to lemon juice or vinegar. Use a specialist cleaning product. If you are stuck, diluted washing-up liquid won't do your marble any harm, and may well remove the stain.

Wood – you'll need to start by dusting, but did you know that a slightly damp cloth is best? It picks up the dust, rather than moving it elsewhere. I also like using the dust-removing attachment on my vacuum cleaner for general dusting. Your mild washing-up liquid formula will work beautifully to treat any general stains on woodwork – just a touch on the stain, wiped away with a damp cloth, will do the trick.

Of course, wood is the very worst for water stains. Try a little bit of olive oil rubbed gently into the wood and left for a good while, or toothpaste, believe it or not! You can rub some white toothpaste into the stain, then wipe it away, before using your normal furniture polish. If the stain is stubborn, try mixing your toothpaste with some baking soda.

If you have lots of rings on your table after a dinner party, try rubbing some Vaseline into them, leave for a good while, then buff gently. The only water-stain treatment that I have yet to try is mayonnaise. I can see why it might work on water stains, because of the oil in it, and it won't do your wood furniture any harm. Apply a liberal coating, leave to soak in, then wipe away.

At the Park Hotel Kenmare, we have a lot of antique furniture that requires special care, and I find that beeswax polish applied and buffed gently is perfect. Every time I use it, I'm reminded of the lavender-scented polish that Mum used to use – I think it was made by Reckitt's. There truly is nothing nicer than the smell of fresh polish!

Most modern furniture nowadays isn't made of solid wood; it tends to be a veneer on a non-solid base, so it's easier to clean and maintain. But, for those of you who have invested in solid-wood kitchen countertops, please don't forget that they need to be oiled. Your kitchen supplier will – hopefully! – have told you this. Mineral oil is what you require and you'll need to oil your countertop about once a month. You'll find it in hardware stores and also in art supply shops.

If you'd like to make your own beeswax furniture polish, try this recipe. You can buy beeswax in blocks or pellets from candle-making suppliers, online or via mail order. All you need is one part beeswax to one part white spirits. You dissolve the beeswax in a bowl over a pot of boiling water – rather like you do when you melt chocolate – then slowly add your spirits until you have a runny solution. When it's cooled, pour it into a jar, and you have beeswax polish!

CATHY'S TIP:

You can make scratches on wooden furniture disappear by applying some shoe polish in the same shade. Rub gently into the scratch and buff to a shine.

Plastic – be careful not to use cream cleansers on plastic surfaces, as they are abrasive and could leave scratches. The best solution here for stain removal is diluted washing-up liquid. If the stain is a bit stubborn, try a paste of baking soda and water. Don't rub it in, just leave it to soak into the stain for a while before wiping away. If this doesn't work, you might need to try a solvent, like nail polish remover or white spirits. Just dab a little on some cotton wool or a paper towel and rub into the stain. Don't spread a lot onto the stain, unless you want to be knocked out by fumes!

Ceramic and other 'new' surfaces, like Corian, slate, granite etc. – the message here is to avoid abrasive, acidic cleaners. Did you know that these surfaces are actually porous, so you could damage them if you go mad with the lemon juice or cream cleanser? Best to use just warm water for daily stains, then a tiny dab of washing-up liquid for tougher stains. If you have a natural stone or granite worktop, or a slate floor, you'll know all about how tricky these surfaces can be – but, on the plus side, all you need is a mop or a sponge and some warm water!

Soapstone – is another work surface that looks lovely, but is actually easier than other 'natural' surfaces to maintain, because it's a bit more durable. Your diluted washing-up liquid is what you need here. Be aware that you'll need to oil soapstone every month or two with mineral oil. Whatever surface you choose, don't let your kids near it, as my sister Kate learned. She'd just had a brand new kitchen installed and she was only delighted with it, until one of her sons took a big chunk out of a worktop while practising his golf swing! The worktop was all of one week old. Her husband Peter, who's very handy, managed to do a repair, but honestly ... why do youngsters always try these things indoors!?

Enamel – all bathtubs used to be enamel, but nowadays, baths can be made out of anything from plastic to stone. As a general rule of thumb, baking soda mixed with water is perfect for getting rid of soap scum on your bathtub. If you have an acrylic finish on your bathtub, washing-up liquid is just the job: one part liquid to four parts water. One trick I learned from my research was that when you apply your cleanser to the tub, leave it for a while. Don't rinse it off immediately, but let it rest while you clean the rest of the bathroom – then rinse and dry with a cloth that won't scratch. You can even fill the bath with water, squirt some washing-up liquid in and leave for the afternoon if your bath is particularly yucky. This solution will also work for enamel bathtubs, but the trick here is not to use bleach, which will stain your lovely enamel. If in doubt, dab a bit of whatever you're using in a hidden place and check to see if it leaves a stain. If not, work away!

WINDOWS AND MIRRORS

I came across this lovely phrase from an old book of household management, *Enquire Within*: 'Dirty windows speak to the passer-by of the negligence of the inmates.' It amused me no end! And the subject of windows reminds me of a gadget I once bought for that purpose. It was the early 1980s and I was staying in London at the Tara Hotel, ably managed by Eoin Dillon. I was in Covent Garden when I heard a lot of roaring and shouting from a man selling this most marvellous window cleaner – magnetic, if you can imagine that, with two bits to it. One for one side of the window with a sponge on it, the other, a magnet. The idea was that you clamped the cleaner on either side of the window – God knows why! It was all the rage at the time and I had to have one. I took it home to my hotel, where I was on the fifth or sixth floor and it stuck together beautifully. I don't know what happened but I must have gone in reverse or something, because the next thing I knew, the outside half of the gadget came clean away and fell five storeys. I hardly dared look! I scanned the papers the next day for news stories about flying window cleaners hitting a baby in its pram or knocking someone off their bicycle. They wouldn't know the half of it, I thought ruefully, putting the remaining half of the gadget into my suitcase and taking it home – I think it's somewhere in the house to this day!

Anyway, for the outside of your windows, a simple mix of washing-up liquid and warm water, applied with a squeegee or sponge will be perfect – take care when washing on heights or glass roofs! For the inside of your windows, there's no need to buy Windolene when vinegar will do the same trick, wiped on the inside of windows and rubbed off with newspaper.

KITCHEN CLEANLINESS

'Best way to get rid of kitchen odours: Eat out', said Phyllis Diller. It's obvious to me that Phyllis wasn't a big fan of domestic life! Many of us live domestic lives, either by choice or out of necessity, so when it comes to cleanliness, the kitchen is most important. It's where we spend so much of our time and where we do some of our most important activities, like cooking and eating (and talking, of course, but thankfully that doesn't come with a hygiene warning).

I spend a lot of my time in the big industrial kitchen at the hotel, so I can fully understand the importance of cleanliness and hygiene, but it's also important on the home front, too. You don't need to be able to eat your dinner off the floor, but a reasonable balance between living and cleanliness is a must. Here are some of my top tips for a clean kitchen:

- **Use a different chopping board for vegetables and meat, to avoid cross-contamination, and wash each board with hot soapy water after using it, giving it a really good scrub, before drying thoroughly. I use heavy plastic chopping boards that are dishwasher safe, so even after scrubbing, I can pop them into the dishwasher to disinfect them.**

- **Use your sink to wash lettuce and veg – not to scrub your muddy trainers, or clean the dog! If you want to do anything other than rinse food – use a mop bucket or plastic basin that you keep handy.**

- Empty your kitchen bin as regularly as you can – not only does this cut down on nasty smells, but keeping mouldy chicken in it is not a good idea, so out to the main bin it goes. Maybe, like me, you'll have one of those handy bins that has different compartments in it for recycling, composting and rubbish. Either way, keep your rubbish bin under control and wipe around it regularly.

- Have you ever had that awful suction as you pull your bin bag out of the bin? Simply drill a couple of holes in the side of the bin – no more vacuum. If you have a stainless steel bin, you can drill a hole in the plastic liner. You can also drill a hole in the bottom, but look out for leaky rubbish bags!

- Sweep the floor after every meal and mop the floor regularly.

- Be careful about tea towels. I can still remember Mum boiling them on the stove – the smell! – nowadays, a very hot wash will take care of those germs, but make sure that you change your tea towels often. I don't wipe my hands in a tea towel after handling chicken or meat though – I use a paper towel and throw it away afterwards, just to be sure. And don't use a tea towel to dry your hands after washing – keep a nice clean hand towel for that purpose.

- Make sure that you wash your hands after you prepare any kind of meat or fish: I often perform this little dance as I try to turn the taps on to wash my hands with my elbow! Better that, though, than to get nasty germs on the taps.

- Of course, you'll all know about cleaning counters from my tips above, but what about kitchen appliances, like the cooker and the fridge? Hands up who has a cooker that has a lovely layer of grease and grime on it? I know, cleaning the cooker can seem like the most unpleasant of jobs, but like so many others, it can be made a bit easier if you do it fairly regularly, rather than a once-a-year, hold-your-nose job! And you don't even have to use foul-smelling oven cleaners: try wiping down your oven with a sponge soaked in vinegar to keep things under control. If your oven requires a bit more of a clean, a good handful of sugar mashed into the top of half a lemon and used as a scourer is just the job – and it smells good!

- The floor should be mopped regularly, of course, which reminds me of Mum again, because it was the last job she did every night, shooing us out of the kitchen and laying pages of newspapers down on the floor.

HOW TO ... WASH YOUR HANDS

Need I say 'wash your hands'? I know that this might seem obvious, but many of us don't actually know how to wash our hands properly. All you need is soap and hot water – no antibacterial wipes, lotions or cleansers. That's it! In fact, I recently came across one of those fascinating 'Ted Talks' on the subject of handwashing, which was a real eye-opener. A public health lady, called Myriam Sidibe made the very good point that so many diseases can be prevented by simple handwashing, and she has been making it her mission to get children to wash their hands before eating and after the bathroom, to reduce child mortality. It's so simple when we think about it, but so necessary.

Wash hands and apply soap.

Rub your hands together.

Interlace your fingers, then wiggle your hands so that in between your fingers is well coated with soap – do this a few times to clean your fingers.

Make sure that the **tops of your fingers and under your nails get a good rub.**

Twist your hands together again and keep rubbing – Steps 2–5 should take 20 seconds.

Give hands **a good rinse.**

Dry thoroughly.

Turn off tap using your tissue/towel.

Speaking of smelling, the fridge is a classic, and even the most innocuous of items can create a nasty stink. So how do you keep your fridge clean and, most importantly, smell-free? Of course, regular cleaning will work, but, more importantly, clear out your fridge. Whenever I do a shop and go to stock the fridge, I do a quick whizz around to see what's in it: that old chutney I bought at the farmers' market, a half jar of olives and the pesto with the lovely furry top! I dispose of all items I simply can't use, and try to get creative with things that I can – the jar of olives can go into pasta, the chutney can adorn my ploughman's lunch or, by the miracle of the internet, can be used in various recipes. But the key is to know when to throw! Many of us, me included, get a bit confused about *best-before* and *use-by* dates – we're not sure what they mean. I consulted the Food Safety Authority of Ireland for pointers. According to them, 'best before' means a 'date of minimum durability'. Well, that cleared that up then! What this means is the date at which a food might not taste, smell or look as good – but might well still be safe to eat. If the item is to be stored at room temperature, like a can or jar, or frozen, you'll see a 'best before' date – some people are happy to eat something that is past this date. If, on the other hand, the item is perishable, chilled or could cause something nasty if not eaten fresh, then 'use by' is the correct term. This means, generally, that the item is considered safe to use until that date and not after. I know this because, running a hotel, we have to be very strict about the correct procedure. Eggs are the only exception, having a 'best before' date stamped onto them.

Storing food in your fridge for maximum hygiene is also very important. At the hotel, we have a rigorous system of storage, for obvious reasons, but it's also important at home, not just to prevent smells, but also to prevent nasty bugs. Things like E. coli, campylobacter, staphylococcus ... I know, they sound terrifying! Basically, these are bugs that can pass to humans from food and cause nasty bugs. Did you know that Ireland has one of the highest rates of E. coli in Europe? That should give us an extra incentive to be clean and to store things properly in the fridge. If you buy a lovely bit of beef and store it on top of some cured ham, it's possible that cross-contamination will occur, so store your beef well away from other foods.

Store it on a plate to catch any leakages, or even better, in a container, and don't place the plate over your vegetable crisper drawer either.

When I was a child, all meat was cooked to within an inch of its life, probably because safe storage was an issue. Many people didn't have refrigerators, so it was important to cook thoroughly. But nowadays we can have a lovely juicy steak or joint of beef that's still pink in the middle, as long as we sear the outside. According to www.safefood.eu, 'Poultry, pork, rolled joints, burgers, sausages, chicken nuggets, kebabs, kidneys, liver and other types of offal, and any meat or fish that has been minced or skewered' needs to be cooked through. 'The reason is that with whole cuts of meat, any harmful bacteria will live on the outside only. But if meat has been minced or chopped up, the bacteria get moved around.' So when you are cooking your chicken stir-fry, you'll need to make sure that you cook the chicken until the juices run clear. And the same goes for a pan full of lovely sausages and, very importantly, for that chilled lasagne that you're reheating. Anything chilled needs to be cooked until it's piping hot all the way through. If you reheat in the microwave, be particularly careful, as you can have some bits that are cooked and others that are still cold. Check your food in a number of spots to make sure that it's hot. Now that I've frightened the life out of you all, here are a few tips for food storage, some of which might surprise you.

- **How many of us store our potatoes and onions together? Well, if you do, they'll go off much quicker, because the onions release gases which will make your potatoes sprout.**

- **And then there's the egg-in-the-fridge, egg-in-the-cupboard debate. Some people swear that eggs taste better if kept in the cupboard, particularly for baking; others feel that this is a shortcut to salmonella! I'm a fridge man myself, but either way, the key is not to keep them in the door, as the changes in temperature when you open and close the door are bad for them. Mind you, I was amused to read a story about a British man who served on nuclear submarines, where the eggs were** stored next to the sonar equipment on their exercises in the Atlantic: 'and would remain perfectly edible throughout the long voyage'. I'm glad I wasn't on that submarine.

- Vegetables can be stored outside the fridge – indeed, many of them do better that way, with the exception of carrots. Onions and garlic can be stored together, in a little basket on the counter. If you store your onions in the fridge, they'll go mushy, but carrots will do very well in the fridge, I find, as will celery. I have tried to store them in my larder, but have ended up with mushy carrots! I am also told that plastic is the enemy of vegetable storage, so take your carrots and celery out of any plastic wrapping. I did see one piece of advice that suggested that I store onions in knotted pairs of tights, which is probably a bridge too far.

- Potatoes need to be stored in a nice dark place to stop them sprouting – and take off that plastic bag. Paper is much better for potatoes.

- Tomatoes will really keep their flavour if you store them outside the fridge. There's nothing more unpleasant than a chilly, watery tomato. If you're lucky enough to have a glut of summer tomatoes from the garden, you can freeze them. Really! They won't work in a salad, but they'll be lovely added to soups and sauces in the winter. Just blanch them quickly in boiling water, drop them into cold water to remove the skins, core and slice them, then freeze. Other veg that freeze well are courgettes, green beans, peas and sweetcorn. Many people also swear by frozen fresh herbs. Again, you might not use these in a salad, but they will be perfect added to soups and sauces.

If you have a larder, do an inventory every couple of weeks. Remove old jars and bottles – there's no room for that dusty bottle of ouzo that Aunty Mary brought back from Greece! – and place items that need to be eaten sooner at the front of your larder, so that you use them first. Store pasta, rice and flour in lidded containers, because of the risk of weevils. These little bugs love dried goods. One handy tip suggested adding a bay leaf to the jar, because the bugs don't like it.

THE SPRING CLEAN

I like the quote, 'I feel like I need to clean the house, so I'm going to lie down until the feeling passes.' Unfortunately, when you wake up, the house will still be dirty! I'm also very fond of Quentin Crisp's famous quote about cleaning his New York flat: 'There's no need to do any housework at all. After the first four years, the dirt doesn't get any worse.'

These little quotes might seem silly, but they have meaning nowadays, when you might well wonder who on earth has the time for a full spring clean. It's not like my mother's day, when she lived in Sligo and had to get the house ready for the 'Stations'. These weren't the Stations of the Cross, but the name marked when it was your turn in the community to host Mass in your home, followed by a meal for everyone. You can imagine the fuss that caused, and sometimes things would get out of hand! Thankfully, your turn would only come around every few years. It wasn't a bad psychology, in fairness, to clean your house thoroughly in expectation of a visitor.

In our time-pressed world, there are any number of companies offering spring-cleaning services, but they can't declutter for you, or decide whether you really need two jumpers of the same colour, or whether to repair or ditch your favourite pair of shoes, or be delighted when you find that long-lost earring down the back of the sofa; spring cleaners can *clean*, and you might feel a sense of relief at that, but I'll bet you'll feel a real sense of satisfaction if you do it yourself. Cleaning isn't just about cleaning – it's about getting on top of things, feeling that the everyday isn't taking over your life. Or, why not look on it as spring cleaning for your soul as well as your home? Time spent doing mindless activities like cleaning frees up the mind to think of other things. Agatha Christie used to plot her novels while washing the dishes, so anything's possible!

However, now that the spring clean isn't so much of an annual ritual, you might need to set yourself goals to get that cleaning done. Maybe you want to host a party at home, or invite guests to stay, but you feel that you can't until you have a really good tidy. Maybe you have simply accumulated too much clutter and you want to experience the 'joy', as Marie Kondo puts it, of a tidy home. I'll look at decluttering and tidying in the next chapter, but the point I'm making is that you'll need a carrot – or a stick! – to motivate yourself to clean.

Once you've established your goals, it's time to make some kind of a plan. Are you going to tidy/clean room by room, or are you going to tackle things in a certain order – rugs, curtains, surfaces, floors, appliances and so on? I like a room-by-room method, as it reminds me of my mother's spring cleaning when I was a child. I'd come home from school to find the doors and windows of the elected room open to let in the air, and Mum wiping everything down with a mixture of washing-up liquid and vinegar.

But before we go any further, make your spring clean a family affair. If you live in a shared house with friends or family, there's no reason for one of you to be breaking your back cleaning while everyone else sits in front of the telly! Make sure everyone is 'on board' and apportion tasks or rooms accordingly.

Next, get your cleaning materials together, whatever you think you'll need, from the hoover with the cobweb-removing attachment to your mop and bucket, as well as your cleaners, whether you choose 'traditional' ones like vinegar or baking soda, or modern ones. If you do opt for modern cleaners, try to find ones that won't fill the place with chemical fumes. Many hardware stores and supermarkets have lines of non-harmful, eco-friendly cleaners. Your cleaners might include: baking soda, vinegar, lemon juice, beeswax – these will cover most of the tasks in your clean. Feel free to use 'stronger' products if you prefer.

You might also need:

- **A stepladder to reach awkward spots.**

- **A selection of bin liners for rubbish, ziplock bags for things you find that you'd like to keep together, and a box or tub for 'random' things you come across that you'll need to find a place for.**

- **Bulldog clips – I have a drawer full of these, because I find them fantastic for clipping together open packets of sugar, flour, spices etc.**

- A roll of recycled kitchen paper.

- Old tea towels or washcloths for wiping and dusting.

- A sweeping brush and a dustpan and brush.

- Washing-up liquid.

- A small bucket for rinsing and washing.

- A hand-held vacuum cleaner, if you have one – these are great for giving a quick vacuum as you go, so you don't have to lug the big Hoover around.

- Rubber gloves.

- A scrubbing pad.

- A roll of white office labels, for labelling spice jars, rubbish, recycling etc.

Once you have your materials assembled, make a list of the jobs that need doing in each room. So, for example, a kitchen spring clean might look something like the below.

KITCHEN CLEANING CHECKLIST

- Vacuuming the skirting boards, ceiling, corners, air vents, window ledges, behind the radiator – all of the places that normally get forgotten.

- Wiping the top of the cooker hood, top of the cupboards, fridge, freezer – again, the dusty corners that no one sees.

- Decluttering your kitchen cupboards, throwing out jars and packets that are past their sell-by dates; reorder your spice rack – fill the little spice jars, instead of leaving your spices in their packets; remove any crockery that's broken or chipped, or that no longer matches.

- Buying drawer organisers or dividers can really help to restore order to that jumble of spoons, potato mashers, garlic presses, sieves etc. that you have piled in a heap in a drawer.

- Buying sealed jars or boxes to store flour, pasta, cereal and other dry goods, so that they don't spill – and label them so the 'sniff' test won't be necessary to see what's in them!

- Removing the blinds or window coverings from the window and cleaning them.

- Cleaning the fridge, cooker and freezer and throwing out any old food; give your dishwasher a run with one of those rinsing tablets, having first cleaned out the food trap.

- Emptying the toaster of crumbs and cleaning the coffee maker; empty the breadbin and give it a really good wash, ensuring that you dry it thoroughly.

- Checking your smoke alarm, carbon-monoxide detector and fire extinguisher to make sure that any batteries work.

- Wiping around light fittings.

- If you have any photos of the kids or artwork on the fridge, now is a good time to – tactfully! – replace them with newer achievements; if you have a prize or a medal that one of your children is particularly proud of, but that's looking the worse for wear, see if you can frame it or laminate it to make it last longer.

- Dusting the leaves of any plants in the kitchen and giving them a little TLC (some plant food and water).

- Cleaning the splashback and walls – kitchen walls can have food and drink splashes on them, so a really good clean will make them sparkle (and don't forget door handles).

- Finishing with a really good scrub of the kitchen floor; if you have tiles, make sure you use the correct cleaner.

You can adopt the same forensic approach to any of the rooms in your house – for example, the living room, removing any curtains or blinds to give them a really good clean and removing any mildew or mould from them. You could remove your – hopefully – washable sofa covers and wash them, taking the cushions off the sofa to give it a really good vacuum – you'll probably discover all kinds of things lurking under the cushions! If you have a leather sofa, use a specialist leather cleaner to polish it to a shine. And don't forget to pull it away from the wall to hoover underneath. Steam clean any rugs or carpets, *paying close attention to any care instructions*. If you have a TV set – take care with cleaning. Don't let loose on your plasma TV set with anything other than a soft cloth, and LCD screens also need a special cleaner. Your TV or computer store will know what you should use to get rid of any tricky blobs or stains.

Before you begin your spring clean, think about having a good clear-out. After all, there's no point in spring cleaning if you are overwhelmed with stuff and can't find a clear space. My decluttering tips follow, but the key is to be prepared with everything you'll need; to share out the tasks so that you don't feel overburdened; to find ways to stay motivated so that you don't give up halfway; and to give yourself a nice reward at the end. You deserve it!

KEEPING A PET-FRIENDLY HOME CLEAN

We had a budgie called Joey, who used to perch on our shoulders, and we loved him, even though we hated cleaning the cage! We had no dogs – at least, not for long. We did have a Yorkie at one stage, but the poor thing was gone in three weeks. He was a friendly fellow, but he had a habit of jumping up on us, and as I had calipers at the time, Mum wasn't a bit keen on this. So, the Yorkie went – to relatives, I hasten to add, so we saw him from time to time – but we never had a dog again.

My lifestyle nowadays means that a dog would be out of the question, but we have actually kept horses at the hotel, and we even tried alpacas, but they didn't work, because they kept spitting at the guests! Our greatest pet success was the two Falabella miniature horses we bought from a man in Northern Ireland years ago. They aren't ponies, by the way, but tiny horses, and they were bred in Chile by a Count Falabella to go down the salt mines. We thought they'd make a lovely addition to the hotel garden and indeed they did – the guests loved them. But the manner of their arrival was less than ideal!

We were making our purchase at the height of the Troubles and this lovely man from 30 miles north of Newry volunteered to drive the horses down for the princely sum of 30 pounds. All the way down to Kerry in a horsebox – what a bargain, I thought. They were to come on a Friday in February, but our field wasn't fenced in, so a staff member, Gerry, said he'd put them in a shed on his farmyard. I'd arranged with Michael, one of the boys in the staff house, to be there with me when they arrived. So we were all set.

It was a dreadful night, I remember, pouring out of the heavens, as this Northern Irish car came up the drive. The driver rolled down the window and smiled. 'I never knew that Kerry was so far from Newry,' the man said. It had taken them nearly 12 hours to get here! I directed him up to the Horseshoe pub to get a quick meal before closing, offering him my car, and Michael and myself went to head up to Gerry's. I'd rung ahead, but Gerry's mother told me that he'd gone 'shining', which, for those of you who don't live in the country, means chasing after foxes with a big torch.

Michael and I took off, in the Northern Irishman's car, pulling the horsebox up into the Kerry mountains in the pouring rain, which, as you can imagine, was a journey and a half, but after many twists and turns, we found the farm, and I sent Michael off to get some rope to tether the little horses. Daddy Falabella was taken out of the horsebox first, but his poor son was frantic at this stage. The poor little thing leapt out, and it was all I could do to grab him by the mane. Even though he was tiny he was jumping all over the place, and next thing I knew, I'd ripped a huge hole in my three-piece suit! (I had been at work, so was not dressed appropriately.)

Soaking wet and bedraggled, we set off with the little horses towards the shed at the far side of farmyard, but what did we see when we got to the gate only a farmyard filled with about two thousand sheep, between us and the shed. We had to navigate our way through this sea of sheep – and the little fellow, by now half-mad with fright, started to jump over them, knocking them in the head in his attempt to find his dad. I can hardly believe that we eventually got them into the shed.

By this stage, Gerry's dad, a very elderly man, had come out. He insisted on inviting me into the house, while Michael went in search of hay for the Falabellas. In I went into the kitchen and Gerry's dad banged on the ceiling with a broom. 'Get up, get up.' He was waking his wife to come down and make a cup of tea, having probably not made a cup of tea in his life. In the meantime, I was offered a big glass of whiskey. Of course, I don't drink, so that was a little awkward, not to mind the fact that I was their son's boss, so the conversation was a bit stilted. And where on earth was Michael, I began to wonder, after 20 minutes stretched to half an hour. Surely it couldn't take that long to get a bit of hay? Eventually, Michael came back and was offered a glass of whiskey, which he drank, while I contented myself with a cup of tea, before deciding it was time enough to be going.

When we got outside, I said, 'Where the hell were you?'

'The sheep are down for the ram, and when I went into the hay barn the ram was there, and he kept running for me. I had to protect myself with a bale of hay,' he explained. It was not our night! Eventually, we turned the car and horsebox around and made for home, where we spotted our Northern Irish friends returning. They looked very happy. 'People are very nice,' they exclaimed. 'They all talk to us in the Free State.'

We had those two little horses for 25 years, until Daddy sadly died of 'sweet itch', a blood infection caused by insect bites We sent his son to the local stables, where the children loved him and he was happy as Larry. I'm not sure what the moral of the story is here!

So, as you can see, I fully understand people's adoration of their pets. But pets and nice clean homes do not go together. This is fine if you're not too bothered about dog hairs on the sofa or, as in the case of a friend of mine, a cat who has taken up residence in the bathroom sink!

It is possible to have pets and keep your home in reasonably good shape, but you need to work a bit harder. Some of you might say that you also have to lower your standards, but I'll leave that up to you!

If you're a dog owner, you might not get terribly excited about muddy paw prints on the kitchen floor, but I'm sure you still want to maintain basic standards of hygiene, especially if you have little people in the house too. We love our doggies, but if you have one, you'll probably have heard about toxocariasis – basically worm eggs that live on dog faeces and can cause blindness in humans. There's tapeworm, of course, and salmonella, and with cats, toxoplasmosis, which is very dangerous for pregnant women. Not to mention the risk of allergies – it's a wonder we keep them at all!

However, if you follow a few basic rules, life with your furry friends can be happy and safe.

DO

- **Wash your hands after touching, playing with or feeding pets.**

- **Empty your cat's litter tray every second day at the very least.**

- **Wash your pet's bedding once a week. If this sounds like a lot, think of what might be lurking in the dog basket. Buy an easy-clean rug or cushion that can be washed frequently and put this rug wherever Fido likes to rest. You can then pick it up and throw it in the washing machine.**

- **Hoover up areas where your dog or cat has been regularly. If you sprinkle baking soda on particularly smelly areas and wait for a while, before hoovering up, it gets rid of doggy smells.**

- **Get a vacuum cleaner with a HEPA (High Efficiency Particulate Arrestance/Air) filter. This means that it can suck up more airborne particles. The problem with pets is often not actually their hair or fur, but their dander, or tiny flecks of skin that come off as they roam – and their saliva, which contains dander from all that licking they do. The best way to tackle dander, which quickly becomes airborne, before landing on the floor and other surfaces, is to vacuum, dust and wipe surfaces regularly.**

- **Keep the kitchen floor clean if your pets walk across it. Remember, they bring in all kinds of dirt from outside, so mop regularly. A friend of mine who is a dog owner dips her dog's paws in a basin of lukewarm water after winter walks to wash off mud. Another tip is to buy hypoallergenic wipes to clean little paws – more expensive, but handy in a bind.**

- Wash your pet's feeding bowls frequently.

- Brush and wash your dogs frequently to keep dander to a minimum. Brush your dog outside so that all that hair will stay outside – if you can wash your dog outside, all the better.

- Did you know that your cat might sometimes need a bath? I can hardly believe that I'm even writing this, but apparently, they do! Most short-haired cats are fine, but if your kitty has rolled in something unpleasant, has long hair, or is overweight (and can't reach all of the way down to clean), an occasional bath might be necessary. As cats tend to dislike baths, make sure that you have a willing assistant and that all of your bathing equipment is close at hand, and do it quickly. Check with your vet first, though, before undertaking any home bathing.

DON'T

- Let your pet lick you, particularly near your mouth. I know that Fido likes to give kisses, but don't indulge him. You are probably well aware of where his mouth has been, so all the more reason to just pat him on the head.

- Prepare your pet's meals on the kitchen counter.

- Let cats use anything other than a litter tray for doing their business. Cats like digging up soil and using window boxes, flower beds and other inconvenient places. I have found that placing wooden barbecue skewers a few inches apart in my window boxes and flower beds deters them.

- Let him or her run loose on the furniture. I know that some people like having their pets in bed with them – Heaven help us – or don't mind dogs sprawled on the sofa. Decide in what areas you are happy to let your pets roam and stick with them. Make the rest out of bounds. This is probably easier said than done, but persist. I have a friend who spent a morning training her dog not to sit on the back of the sofa. He liked this spot because it was up high, but developed a superiority complex and growled every time she approached him! She persisted in telling him 'down' every time he jumped up – so, rest assured, if you are consistent, Fido will get the message! On the other hand, if you are happy to let your pets onto the sofa, make sure that it has a washable cover that can be easily removed.

- Let your dog or cat wee on the carpet. Accidents will happen, though, so get to them quickly. Make a solution of washing-up liquid and lukewarm water – about half a teaspoon to a mug of water – and apply to the stain, blotting carefully with paper towels. If the wee is particularly pungent, you might need to apply a specialist carpet cleaner to the stain.

- Let your cat spray the neighbour's front doorstep. This is a common occurrence, so be a good neighbour and if you have any complaints, spray any popular areas with a cat-deterrent spray (it can be bought from your hardware store, but will need to be refreshed after the rain). Cat-deterrent sprays have a smell that our feline friends don't like. Alternatively, a sprinkle with vinegar might deter them.

- Let your cat or dog spray food all over the floor. Dogs in particular can be messy eaters, so put a wipe-clean mat under his or her bowl, which you can then lift and wash.

CLEANING YOUR CAR

I spend a lot of time in my car – I mean, a lot! I am constantly driving between meetings, filming of *At Your Service*, and up and down to Sligo to see my mother. I couldn't do it if my car was a mess. I often have to carry spare shirts and suits for filming, as well as an overnight bag, and I want them to stay clean.

Whether or not you're a car enthusiast, you'll want a clean automobile, but this becomes all the more important if your car will be full of children or pets, or even sports equipment. Your lovely car will face special challenges then!

The first rule of thumb is to keep the clutter at bay. With children and pets, the car can quickly become full of muddy boots, half-eaten sandwiches, pencils, little toys, old books and all sorts of other 'stuff'. So, rather than doing a big purge once a month, tidy your car every day. Yes, that's right! If you do a quick once-over every day after you come home from work or doing the shopping, you can avoid the creeping mess that we find so unpleasant.

When you step out of the car, get the kids to take their clutter with them – ask them to remove schoolbags, coats and sports kit and to put them away in the house. Remove any old recyclable coffee cups and rinse them, popping them in the recycling bin, then pick up rubbish and pop it in the car rubbish bin that you've bought – or the simple supermarket plastic bag that you've kept in the car for just such a purpose – and, hey presto! If you spot any spills, clean them now, and if you don't, a quick wipe of door handles and window ledges with a baby wipe is just the ticket. And you're done!

Having somewhere to store the clutter can be a boon in a family car. If you are constantly on the road between school and after-school classes, you will accumulate a lot of clutter, so have some tidies at the ready. You can buy car storage pockets online that fit on the back of the driver's seat, and you can also repurpose an old shoe tidy, or indeed one of those TV remote control holders, which I have seen neatly fitted under a child's car seat, with all of their little pencils and books at their fingertips. However, many purpose-made car-seat organisers are specially designed to hook under the seat of the car and are pretty cheap – so keep an eye out for one that will fit your seat. You can also keep a spare cardboard box or plastic laundry basket/box in your boot for any shopping emergencies – or indeed, to use as a bin if you are going on a long journey. You can buy a shelf on legs for the boot – if you have a big boot that is – allowing you to store things on two levels.

This isn't strictly speaking a tidying matter, but while I remember it, every car should have a first-aid kit and a car emergency kit, with jump leads, a tow rope and one of those bright red reflective triangles in case you break down. I have jump leads in my car and I've lost count of the amount of times I've lent them to people – I don't mind at all, but it does make me think that they are an essential piece of car kit.

Many of us clean the outside of our cars regularly, taking them to the car wash and buffing them to a lovely shine with car wax, but what about the inside of the car? Whether you have leather or synthetic upholstery, it can be a minefield of grime!

If you have a baby seat, you will be well aware of how much dirt and bits of old food can get lodged beneath it – yuck! You can buy a child's car seat protector from your auto store, or you can make one of your own if you are handy. All you need to do is remove it and hoover it, rather than having to clean out old stains and muck from your good car upholstery.

If your interior is leather – please, please use a proper car leather cleaner. They are designed specifically for cleaning leather in cars, so don't be tempted to use anything else. If your upholstery is synthetic, you can use a number of car or fabric shampoos. Here are a few handy hints for cleaning your car's interior:

- Vacuum first. Like me, you might need to use an extension cable so that your vacuum cleaner reaches far into the car – but be careful. No lugging it out into the rain or dropping it into a puddle! Lift out all floor carpets and give them a good beating. We don't have carpet beaters any more, more's the pity, but give them a good wallop and a shake before vacuuming.

- Be careful about using water on car upholstery, as it will often stain or damage it. If simple 'freshening' is all you need, a sprinkle with baking soda will help. Sprinkle on liberally, leave to absorb nasty smells, then vacuum thoroughly.

- Look carefully at the carpet or upholstery to see if any of it needs stain treatment. Be careful about treating any kind of leather interior – the leather has often been dyed and will run. Test a hidden area first to be sure. Spray the affected areas with a cleaner made for car upholstery, or make one of your own, using a quarter of a cup of baking soda mixed with a cup of water – but don't spray on the upholstery generally, just use it on stained spots. Apply the mix and brush it gently with an old toothbrush, leave for a bit, then blot with kitchen paper, before leaving to dry. If stains are particularly ingrained, a solution of one part vinegar to four parts water with a splash of washing-up liquid will be more vigorous. You can use a little mist of this solution on your synthetic car upholstery. Don't soak it, just spray gently, then rub the seats clean, before leaving to dry thoroughly. You can use window cleaner on the interior and exterior windows ... but did you also know that it works wonders on plastic upholstery? Give it a try!

- Soda water is just the job for applying to – ehm – vomit! I know, but such things are part of life in cars, particularly with queasy kids. Cover the stain liberally with soda water, but don't rub in, just mop and dab until the stain has lifted, before applying your normal fabric cleaner.

- When you are cleaning the inside of your car, don't forget areas like the space between the dashboard and the windscreen, the steering wheel, the drinks container and the glove compartment. Use cotton buds if you need to get into tricky spots.

- Window cleaner also makes a great cleaner of car lights. Just spray and dry off – and your lights will beam brightly.

- Have a packet of baby wipes handy in the car to wipe away sticky things, to keep the steering wheel clean and for any little messes made by child or pet.

- You can make your own car-washing liquid by mixing a quarter of a cup of baking soda and washing-up liquid into two litres of water. Mix well and use when your car needs a good wash.

- You can wash the inside of your windscreen with diluted washing-up liquid – just a dash squirted into warm water will be perfect. Once you have cleaned thoroughly, use a bit of window-cleaning spray to finish – you will finally be able to see through your windscreen!

Car pongs can really hang around. With anything from spilled milk to takeaway food, cars can harbour smells for a long time after their source has been removed. (Just a tip here: if you eat takeaway food in your car, any salt that has been sprinkled on it will damage your chrome – so eat at your peril!)

The worst smell I've ever had in a car came from spilt milk, but the reason why it spilled is a story in itself. When I was fresh out of catering college, I catered for a silver wedding party at the Garda Club in Inchicore in Dublin. It all went very well, and of course we had to tidy up and bring everything home after. I went around and emptied all of the milk jugs on the table into a saucepan, which I placed in Dad's car, an Opel Caravan as I recall, which I'd borrowed for the night. My sister Kate and Tony Forshaw, a friend of mine, had come along to help out and we squeezed into the car along with all of our bits and bobs from the party – and the saucepan of milk. We were waiting at the traffic lights between Kilmainham and Inchicore in two lanes of traffic, when I spotted a Mini flying towards us down the hill. He indicated, but too late, and hit us broadside on. We were pushed into the car on the inside lane and both doors of our car were mangled. When I eventually clambered out through the window, what did I see, only a river of milk flowing down the hill. The saucepan had upended! My poor father could not get the smell of milk out of the car and actually had to sell it a month later, because he couldn't stomach the smell. I don't think there's anything worse than spilt milk in a car!

Many of us will use the cardboard trees or diffusers that plug into cigarette lighters and they are fine, but what about more persistent smells? Firstly, you need to try to eliminate the source of the smell. This you can do by cleaning your upholstery thoroughly, as above. Then, try spraying it liberally with upholstery spray and leaving it for a while to soak in; the same can be done with a good sprinkling of baking soda. Again, leave for a while to absorb odours, then hoover up. If you've ever used sachets of activated charcoal to get rid of pongs in shoes, did you know that they work equally well in cars? Stick a few bags around the car to absorb unpleasant smells.

Cigarette smoke is particularly hard to get rid of as the smell really lingers. You'll need to spray deodoriser into the vents of the car and into the car's intake valve, as well as emptying ashtrays regularly and cleaning the inside of the windscreen, where many smoke deposits land. Check your car manual carefully to see where the intake valve is, before you go spraying deodoriser where it shouldn't be sprayed!

A little bag of coffee grounds is also a good DIY home freshener, if you like the smell of coffee, and it's a good neutraliser of other odours. You could also soak make-up pads or cotton balls in essential oils, before placing them in various spots around the car – they won't last for ever, but they do smell nicer than the ready-made fragrancers.

If you must buy air fragrancers, try ones that clip to your air vents, to neutralise pongs. You can also buy a plug-in air purifier, if you feel that air purifiers have proven benefits. I was amused to come across a few food-flavoured air fresheners during the course of my research, such as popcorn, and my favourite, a bacon-flavoured air freshener, which emits the smell of sizzling bacon!

CHAPTER TWO

Tidiness is Next to Godliness

'Have a place for everything and keep the thing somewhere else; this is not a piece of advice, it is merely a custom.'

MARK TWAIN

As I write, I'm doing a big 'clear out' in my home in Kerry and I'm trying to come up with a plan of action, so you can consider me a guinea pig for what I'm about to write about tidying! For a start, I have 250 coffee table books, piled under the table in the sitting room, because I've nowhere else to put them, not to mention my wardrobe, full of suits, sweaters, shirts and ties. Once I donated some lovely silk ties to the local charity shop in Kenmare and saw one of them tied to the gate in a field one day when I was passing in the car. I didn't know whether to be amused or insulted!

In truth, I probably don't provide the best example of a streamlined home, because I find it hard to throw things out, but I've enlisted my sister Kate to help me because, quite honestly, the task seems overwhelming. I've also consulted some of the many books on tidying and decluttering and have learned one simple rule: break it down. Don't try to tidy everything up in one go and fall in an exhausted heap on the living room floor (what's left of it, under the mess!). Take it step by step and you'll feel that you're getting there. And be realistic about what you can achieve in the time allotted. Say you have a day off and you are determined to get the house in order. Don't try to whirl around the whole place like a dervish – pick, say, the bathroom and get that into tip-top shape, then sit back and admire it and make some time for yourself. Kate and I plan to go room by room, for example, so that we can enjoy our lovely clean kitchen or guest bedroom, before tackling the next room, and so on. Here goes!

CLUTTER

Let's start with a word that none of us likes – clutter. I think that it plays a big psychological part in our lives, from the shirts we wore when we were much younger and slimmer, which we keep in case we miraculously return to our 20-year-old selves, to our GAA medals, relics of our youthful successes, to things that we hang on to because we must get round to reading/listening to them. Either way, when it comes to clutter, we tend not to live in the moment, do we? We hang on to that violin from our failed attempt to learn the instrument in case it 'might come in useful' for the kids or a friend. Not very positive! We have a big box in the attic full of wedding presents that we didn't like, but weren't brave enough to donate them; we have old love letters, even though their sender has long gone. It's easy to see why clutter weighs us down – physically and psychologically.

My mother's generation had fewer opportunities to accumulate 'stuff'. As you can see, life was much simpler then. People really didn't have a lot. No gadgets, no remote-control devices – that kind of thing. They had only one set of china, which had been a wedding present and lived in a china cabinet in the sitting room, and clothes were bought twice a year, for summer and winter, and were mended over and over again. Remember your 'good coat', which you were only allowed to wear on special occasions?

Now, before you start, I'm not suggesting that 'the good old days' were better, but there's no doubt that we didn't fill our houses with tons of stuff. If you're like me, you'll have accumulated plenty of it over the years. Along with the things that we hoard for psychological reasons, we also collect stuff as part of modern life – we are a consumer society after all. You might not have received a coffee table book from almost every hotel in the world like me, but you'll probably have CDs that you no longer play because you now download music, a collection of obsolete video tapes, a coffee machine that you can't get around to fixing, or an exercise bike gathering dust in the spare room. Your children might have got a ton of presents for their birthdays and you haven't a clue where you'll fit them all in. You might have tons of photographs in their envelopes in a drawer or – Mum's favourite – an old biscuit tin. You might have a broken food processor hidden behind your new one in the kitchen cupboard, because you don't want to throw it out, in case it comes in handy. Well, it won't, I can tell you. Life will be so much more relaxing if we don't have to trip over clutter all the time. I think we'd free ourselves up a lot, both mentally and physically, if we just got rid of things.

I'd like to think that decluttering could become a habit for us, once we get into it. But how on earth do we get started? Most of us can't even bear to look at the pile of correspondence in the cupboard, or the big tangle of sports equipment in the shed. Well, for a start, it's 'do as I say, not as I do' – declutter regularly, at least every couple of months, because otherwise that stuff will really accumulate. Most of us say that we can't make time, but if we do little and often, that mountain of clutter will shift, and we can use the changing of the seasons to do a larger clear-out. So get your bin bags, cardboard boxes and maybe a big plastic box ready, enlist a willing helper, put some upbeat music on and get started!

I think that a lot of the issues with hanging on to things come from overthinking, so my first suggestion would be to stop! Don't think for a few moments. Go around your living room and select random objects, dividing them into 'keep', 'donate' or 'dispose of'. Follow your first instincts and don't second-guess yourself, even if you've selected Aunty Maeve's silver tea service as a 'dispose of'. Your instincts are usually good – if you don't have any use for it and it's taking up space, it's time for it to go. For me, the key is to try to take the emotion out of things, at least for this little exercise. Imagine that you are an estate agent, assessing what needs to go when a home is being prepared for sale.

Now that you have your stuff separated into three lovely piles, look carefully at each one: the 'dispose of' pile will be easy: duplicate TV remotes from long-lost DVD recorders, the ancient printer or TV set, a broken chair that you have never – and will never! – get around to fixing; old magazines, books and newspapers, damaged china that is beyond repair, broken toys, etc. These will be thrown out or recycled, checking carefully first what your local council will take, so that you avoid just throwing everything into a landfill, which is bad for the environment. Many local councils have book banks, where local charities will collect unwanted books, or clothes banks (see more about recycling in my chapter devoted to that subject, and also below). Some bring centres also have a place for unwanted furniture to be collected by a charity that specialises in making them good as new.

The 'keep' pile will also be relatively straightforward. I think we have an emotional attachment to objects that we use a lot and that are essential to us. It seems silly to be unable to do without our favourite wooden spoon or measuring cup, but objects often carry with them emotions and memories. I have a measuring cup that belonged to my mother, a big silver thing with imperial measurements notched on the surface – 'flour', 'sugar', 'suet' and so on, as well as for liquids. That cup is an essential part of my kitchen and I'd never be without it. I'm sure a digital weighing scales would be much more accurate, but it wouldn't mean as much to me at all. So that cup is never going! I think we know which objects we are really attached to, the ones that mean a lot to us.

The only grey area is the 'give away', and this is often where we get stuck. Take a good look at each item in this category and ask yourself why you are hanging onto it. The word 'guilt' often comes up here! Say Aunty Maeve gave you a vase for your wedding, but you hate it. I bet you still have it because you feel that poor Aunty Maeve saved up for that present and meant the very best when she gave it to you. Of course she did, but you still hate it! If Aunty Maeve is not a frequent visitor, maybe someone else would really like that vase. If you haven't actually done that planned half marathon in the last four years, be honest: you will not be using the exercise bike; if looking at the impulse-bought juicer makes you guiltily vow that you'll use it from now on, the chances are, you'll do exactly the opposite! Getting rid of good old Irish guilt can certainly clear the mind. If, however, you've been looking for something for ages, and then fall upon it, unable to believe that it has been lurking at the back of a cupboard for all that time, there's a sign that it's a useful object.

I was struck by what tidying guru Marie Kondo said about tidying needing to be done in a particular order: 'clothes, books, papers, *komono* (miscellany) and finally, sentimental items' . The reason for this, she says, is that if we come across a much-loved photo stuck in the back of a drawer, we'll spend hours poring over it, reminiscing, instead of getting on with the matter at hand. She has a point, as coming across items of sentimental value does make us stop for a bit; I think that there's something nice about finding some much-loved object or photo that makes the tidying process that bit more bearable, but it is distracting – put it in a box marked 'sentimental value' and resolve to have a good look at it later. I did read about one lady who got so carried away with the 'KonMari' method that she got rid of her kettle and her toaster, which I think is a bit extreme! The point is that once you start, hopefully decluttering will become a habit.

DISPOSING, DONATING AND RECYCLING

So you've gone through your appointed room or the whole house and separated your 'stuff' into piles. What next? Set yourself a strict deadline for getting rid of the 'junk', or else you will simply spend the next few months tripping over it in the hall – or worse, deciding to move things from the 'dispose of' pile to the 'keep' pile – a no-no!

A friend of mine who lived in town used to eagerly await the weekly visit of the 'rag-and-bone' man – remember him? He used to do a trot through her neighbourhood in his horse-drawn cart with a lovely flat bed and collect unwanted washing machines, broken TV sets, and other things. The rag-and-bone man was really useful – I wonder if anyone still gets a visit from him?

Many people nowadays donate to charity shops and this is fantastic for most items, like jewellery, china, pairs of shoes, books, CDs, DVDs etc. However, they won't take pillows or mattresses and some of them don't take toys. This is particularly tricky as so many families have old toys to donate – but check online, as some will accept washed soft toys, and other toys in good order with no loose parts. Mind you, I did read an article in the newspaper a while ago, which informed me that three-quarters of Irish parents threw out their children's toys before Christmas without telling them – and only a quarter of the children actually noticed! I think that this puts things in perspective …

Nowadays, you will need to check if your local council is planning a junk collection, to see if you can leave your stuff out on the pavement. Unwanted washing machines and other white goods are less of an issue: the person delivering your new machine is obliged to take the old one in exchange (for more on this, see Chapter 6). If you are paying a trip to a big store, they will dispose of your old machine in exchange for a new one – but did you also know that larger stores will take any small electrical appliance off your hands, and you don't even have to buy anything! See Chapter 6 for further details.

The WEEE recycling initiative will take care of your old mobile phones, batteries, fridges, freezers, lighting and computer equipment for free, and they have handy drop-off points if you don't have a bring centre near you – see weee.ireland.ie for details.

Look out for collections from your local council too – check their websites for collection days. I had a friend who put out a nice little table and a chair that she'd inherited but that didn't fit her home, the night before a council collection. It vanished within the hour! No harm, she thought, and she still wonders which of her neighbours is enjoying granny's side table! The point I'm making is that what you might consider 'junk' is someone else's treasure, so don't be afraid to get rid of things that don't work for you. True, some people feel a bit uneasy about seeing their nice green cardi on someone else, two weeks after they donated it (and there's always me and the silk ties, as a lesson). If you can, think that your old stuff will benefit someone else and give them pleasure. You might even make some money, which will go towards all the nice storage solutions you'll buy for your home.

STORAGE SOLUTIONS

Which brings me nicely on to what you will do with your 'keep' items. No, you will not put them back exactly where you found them! As Mrs Beeton said, 'A place for everything and everything in its place.' And beware of the attic or shed, groaning with stuff that you will never use, or that you think you will bequeath to the next generation.

It's funny how we get caught up in this generational cycle, when it comes to stuff. A friend of mine and I went to a bric-a-brac fair and while we were rummaging around the stalls, we came across some G Plan furniture. Do you remember G Plan? Teak tables with brightly coloured tops and chairs with spindly legs that were all the rage in the 1960s and 1970s. She told me that her parents had desperately wanted some nice, modern G Plan furniture, but they'd been stuck with a house full of heavy Victorian mahogany and couldn't bring themselves to get rid of it. The moral of the story is: the next generation will not need your old stuff! Try not to impose it upon them unless it's worth something.

Oh, and before you put something into the attic, ask yourself why – if you need it, it should be downstairs, if you don't, why are you putting it into the attic? It's time for it to join the 'junk' pile. Once you've given the shelf or cupboard where you found the item a wipe with a slightly damp cloth and let it air, how do you plan to store all of the things you will be keeping? This may seem obvious, but many retailers have really smart, modern-looking storage 'solutions' in which you can place the stuff you really can't bear to be without, but won't be using on a daily basis. Let's break them down into clothes (and shoes), papers and objects, sentimental or otherwise.

Clothes are the main item that people struggle with. Nowadays, you don't buy a 'good suit' to wear to Mass, which will last you the rest of your life – unless you're me, that is! You buy something cheap and off the peg because you don't expect to wear it for ever – and women's fashion is even 'faster', so you can imagine the strain it puts on our poor wardrobes. Because clothes are so cheap nowadays, it's tempting to keep stocking up on fast fashion, but quite apart from ethical concerns, you'll end up with lots of pink jumpers or blue jeans, or outfits that you only wear once, or worse, fashion disasters that you've brought home from the shop and instantly decided that you will never wear them. So, where do you begin when decluttering and storing your clothes?

Many people swear by the same rules that apply to other objects – if you haven't worn it in six months, ditch it. Now, this might apply to some cheap T-shirt you bought for the summer, but what about that gorgeous coat that's too good to wear every day, or that lovely velvet jacket that a friend bought you in Paris? I still have suits in my wardrobe that I bought 40 years ago, because they were expensive at the time and because I still wear them! I have a thing for quality and find that if I look after my clothes, I can wear them for ever; I can understand why people would buy cheap socks, but when it comes to suits, quality really shows, so buy the best that you can afford.

The point I'm making is that you can't just throw your clothes into a big heap and decide to ditch anything that's more than a few months old – 'curating' your wardrobe needs a little thought. You can start by thinking a bit about your own personal style. If you are someone who likes – or needs – to dress formally, like me, you won't want 50 pairs of jeans in your wardrobe; a couple of pairs will do – so you know to zone in on casual wear as an area where you could do a little pruning. If, however, you work in a zippy restaurant or a dot.com business, where casual style is the thing, you won't want a wardrobe full of suits – one will do you for weddings and funerals – but you might want to hang on to your many white T-shirts and your jeans, only throwing out those that are worn or stained.

Concentrate on the person you are, not on the person you want to be. I think lots of us – and I include myself – buy things that we think will make us look more glamorous or chic, but that don't actually suit us. Think about who you are and what you really enjoy wearing, rather than who you think you should be. You'll know deep down that that faux-fur jacket that was fashionable last year just doesn't work for you because it drowns you, so it's time for it to go. When you are disposing of clothes, look at shape, rather than fashion. If you are short, you'll know that droopy sweaters and baggy clothes simply won't suit your shape, but that fitted jackets and skirts will define you more. So ditch the baggy knits! If your wardrobe is full of black jumpers, maybe it's time to prune your collection: maybe you'll feel liberated enough to buy some colour then.

If you're having difficulty whittling down your wardrobe, get a friend to give you honest advice about what suits you and what doesn't. Who knew that tidying out your wardrobe could be such an emotional rollercoaster!

Another thing to consider is dry cleaning. If you've bought something that's lovely, but that you hardly ever wear because you have to spend a fortune in the dry cleaners, ask yourself: do I really, really want the trouble of this cashmere sweater or silk blouse? Will I have the time to wash this jumper by hand and stretch it carefully out to dry every time I want to clean it? If you are a person who just likes to wear fuss-free clothes, or the very idea of constant cleaning brings you out in a rash, consider donating your awkward piece of clothing to someone you know will appreciate it more than you.

The other thing that you'll need to have a good think about when you open those wardrobe doors are the impulse buys. You know exactly what they are, but you don't want to admit to yourself that you will never wear that enormous red hat, or the shoes with heels so high you can't walk in them. You just want to pretend that of course you'll find just the occasion to wear it. And, some of these purchases might have been very expensive – a handbag or pair of shoes that you bought not because you liked them but because they were 'designer'. Thankfully, expensive items can be sold on: there are lots of little shops and designer clothing websites that will sell on your clothes or bags for you, so you won't be out of pocket. And as for the giant red hat ... find a way to laugh at it and at yourself for having bought it. There will be somebody out there who is just dying to wear it, so donate it and try not to feel too guilty about it. When it comes to clothes, we all make mistakes.

CATHY'S TIP

Instead of storing your jewellery where it can't be seen, think of displaying it in pretty tea cups or around a favourite ornament. This is great for your cheap and cheerful buys, particularly necklaces, so they won't get tangled – but lock your good pieces away in a safe place, and store them correctly. You'll need a proper jewellery box with a soft (satin or velvet) interior. Store pieces in separate little compartments to avoid scratches or tangling – and don't mix pearls with gold and so on. You can buy special anti-tarnish strips for silver jewellery online that will keep it bright for longer.

On a final note, during the course of my research, I came across a brilliantly easy idea. Hang all of your clothes on hangers and place the hangers backwards on the rail in the wardrobe – with the top of the hook facing you. When you take the hanger out to wear whatever is on it, replace it facing forwards. If you have any backwards-facing hangers in your wardrobe after six months, donate the item of clothing, because you are not wearing it. I plan to use this handy tip myself, because I know that I can't possibly wear every one of the blue shirts I've bought.

Now, with your inventory complete, and your unwanted clothes bagged up for the charity shop, what are you going to put back into your wardrobe and how will you organise it?

- **You can buy these clever hanging bag and shoe plastic sleeves, with lovely large pockets for your shoes and bags to slot into – and you'll see them immediately.**

- **Instead of shoving scarves or ties into a corner of a drawer, buy cheap drawer dividers and roll your ties or scarves into coils instead of a big knot. If this sounds like more trouble than it's worth, install a towel rail on the inside of the door and hang your scarves from it.**

- **On my travels I've seen all sorts of hangers, including very handy flower-shaped ones – you pull a scarf through each petal, as well as hangers with a number of holes in them – also for scarves. I've seen** belt-holder hangers and tie hangers in a kind of carousel shape. I think I'll get one of these for my tie collection! Some DIY and home-store places have these clever plastic gadgets that hang from a wardrobe rail, with hooks for up to four hangers on them – genius! You can buy hangers with a number of rods that stick out for you to hang anything up to six pairs of trousers, as well as non-slip hangers with a lovely suede-like covering that will hold your delicate garments in place. If you like DIY solutions, ring pulls from drinks cans threaded through the top of your hanger give you an extra 'hook' to hang another hanger off – so you can get two shirts for the price of one, saving on wardrobe space. And don't forget 'over-door' hangers, which fit over the bedroom door, so no drilling required – ideal for your dressing gown.

- The only place you will need the full height of your wardrobe is for your coats, dressing gown or formal wear. Otherwise, if you are hanging skirts, jackets, trousers or shirts, you can double up, by placing – or getting someone else to place – another curtain rail in the middle of your wardrobe.

- I have seen trouser hangers – the wooden ones that you clamp on the top of your trouser legs – also used to hold pairs of boots – very clever.

- Curtain rings are fantastic for hanging shoes, as I'll get to below, but also for hanging anything with a loop on it like shorts or jeans. Don't hang suit trousers this way, though – unless you want to have an oddly shaped rear end under your suit jacket!

- If you have really nice vintage clothes or are a fashionista, consider installing a picture rail and hanging your best finds as 'art' on the wall.

- Don't forget that drawer organisers can be particularly useful for baby clothes, bibs, socks and vests. You can buy ones with lots of pockets, which is ideal, and pop your tiny garments in. And for older people, have you thought that you can use those perspex boxes for jewellery for other things? Scarves socks, buttons, the loose change that you empty out of your suit pocket ...

- If you need to be smartly dressed try assembling your week's outfits on a Sunday night and hang them in the wardrobe. They'll save valuable time when you're in a rush in the mornings. I do this before I go on a trip and it saves loads of time.

- Speaking of boots, *shoes* are a particularly hard thing to store. Hands up who has a big jumble of them at the bottom of the wardrobe? I once saw a 'decluttering' guru suggest that you buy a number of boxes, big enough to fit a pair of shoes in – shoe boxes even! – and label each box with a picture of the relevant shoes stored there. I think that would be just the ticket for fashion fans, but as I have feet of two completely different sizes, it's not for me.

- A series of towel rails attached to the inside of your wardrobe door make for brilliant shoe hangers. They are also useful for hanging jewellery. I also saw a DIY solution, in a series of staggered small curtain poles – or tension rods – fitted into a wardrobe for shoes. The top tension rod was fitted and then the bottom one at a slant, underneath, so that a heeled shoe would fit on. The great thing about tension rods is that you can move them around until your shoe hangs properly off them. If you place your bottom rod at less of an angle, you can store flat shoes also. You can either pop your shoes in, or if you like use curtain rings as hooks for pairs of shoes. I've even seen the kind of moulding that people install below the ceiling used as a DIY shoe tree – good if you have lovely heeled shoes to show off, but maybe not for the smelly trainers. Many wardrobes now come with a little railed shelf for putting shoes, which can be affixed to the wardrobe door, or my favourite, a frame with a series of prongs on it, onto which you pop your shoes. These might look like items from a medieval torture chamber, but they are custom made to fit at the bottom of flat-pack, assemble-yourself wardrobes.

- A shoe hanger – with lots of pockets for your shoes that hangs on the wardrobe rail – is a good idea, and can also be used for rolled-up sweaters that you don't want to damage by stretching them onto a hanger.

- One of the best 'bespoke' shoe-storage solutions I saw was the bottom two steps of stairs, which had been converted into pull-out drawers for shoes. Genius, I thought, because people are most likely to dispense of their shoes at the bottom of the stairs. Another solution was a neat little pull-out drawer inserted under the stairs, which pulled out to reveal rows of shoes and wellies. A brilliant use of tricky under-the-stairs space, for new builds or when you are refurbishing your home.

- Many DIY retailers now stock special shoe cabinets, with doors that open diagonally, into which you slide your shoes. They have the benefit of being narrow enough to fit in even the smallest hall space. A little unit with two baskets in it inside the front door will also do beautifully, if cost is an issue, as will a little bench with shelves underneath – you sit on the bench when you come in, pop your shoes on the shelf underneath and hey presto! The only problem with shoe storage in cabinets is that the cabinet itself can become a magnet for more clutter – old bills, keys etc. That's why I prefer the bench unit, as you can allocate a basket for shoes, one for brollies and another for post – making sure that you check it regularly.

- You can use coat racks for more than just hanging coats: they also make brilliant hangers for pairs of shoes – the wooden ones work beautifully – and they can be bought cheaply in DIY or home stores.

- A repurposed crate or wooden box will work beautifully as shoe storage. I'll be looking at re- and upcycling later, but if you are handy, take an old wine crate, fit two pre-measured bits of 2 x 4 into it in an x shape – you have a shoe box that will store four pairs of shoes – great if space is limited. The same goes for those awkward corner spaces. You can buy a corner unit, or make a slice-of-cake-shaped unit to store shoes, or indeed other things that you need to keep tidy, but close to hand.

- Plastic 'sleeves' are great – you know the kind that hang from your wardrobe rail or from the back of the door, with pockets for all of your 'stuff', like cotton wool, brushes, toiletries, etc; you can also place pairs of flat shoes into them. And don't forget under-bed storage, where you can keep, say, your summer shoes in the winter and vice-versa. (Mind you, I did come across one pull-out drawer under a bed – for a dog bed. No!)

The thing you have to look out for in enclosed shoe-storage units is the smell. There's nothing worse than opening a shoe drawer to be hit with the pong of smelly trainers! Follow these tips for removing shoe odours and you need never suffer social embarrassment again:

- Replace stinky insoles with odour-eating ones – easily bought in the chemist. Well-used insoles are the main reason your shoes smell. You can buy all kinds of insoles nowadays, including bacteria-catching ones, so go to your chemist and shop around.

- Our two old friends baking soda and vinegar can really help. Sprinkle your stinky runners with a spray of white vinegar to neutralise odours. If you have lovely leather shoes – don't do this! Instead, pop baking soda into something porous, like coffee filters, tie in a knot and pop into your shoes for the night. You can also just sprinkle baking soda into your shoes and vacuum it out the next day.

- An essential oil such as lavender or tea tree sprinkled into your trainer insoles will make them smell lovely as well as killing nasty bacteria.

- Some people swear that cat litter is a great shoe de-stinker, which I can believe, as it certainly works for cat smells. Pop it in something porous, like a pair of old tights or your coffee filters again, and leave overnight.

- Rubbing alcohol, also known as isopropyl alcohol, is widely available in the US, but less so here, although many chemists will have it in stock. Dabbed on some cotton wool and rubbed into your stinky trainers, it's another great solution; by the way, it will also do a great job on appliances, such as computers or tape machines – which is why it can also be found in computer stores.

CATHY'S TIP

If you have any of those handy fabric-softening sheets, roll one up and pop it into your shoes – they will smell lovely in the morning!

THE ART OF FOLDING

There's no doubting that the whole business of storage can be made much easier if you learn how to fold your clothes for maximum tidiness while taking up a minimum of space. No, rolling your jumpers into a big ball and shoving them into a drawer doesn't count. I have seen such a thing as a 'laundry folder' – basically a rectangle of plastic onto which you can fold your shirts or T-shirts, before gently pulling it out – but I don't think you need one. If you follow my instructions, you'll be a folding expert!

- For T-shirts, it's simple: fold in half vertically, then tuck the sleeves back onto the fold, before folding in half again horizontally. You can fold into thirds and then stack your T-shirts on top of each other horizontally in your drawers – you'll fit more in that way and you'll be able to see all of your T-shirts at a glance. To be clear, you place a row of folded T-shirts at the open end of your drawer, then place another row on top of that and so on. Imagine how many more T-shirts you can store that way!

- You can fold jumpers by placing them on a flat surface, folding both sides into the middle vertically, then lining up the sleeves along each fold, before folding again horizontally – but did you know that you can store your jumpers horizontally too? Most of us store them on top of each other and then pull everything apart to find the one we want. (I'll talk about how you need to store them to keep them fresh and moth-free later.) If you store them, folded, beside each other in rows, you need never look for a jumper again! You can do the same for socks and underwear, so no more rummaging in the sock drawer for the pair you want. It's so easy, I'm amazed we don't all do it.

- Sock folding is an art in itself. Yes, you heard me right – sock folding! You might think that life is too short, but think of how nice it will be to be able to find pairs of matching socks, or to put your hand on the pair that works with your best suit. I have come across a 'sock folding machine' on my travels, but that's overdoing it! Try this: place your socks in a cross shape on a flat surface, i.e. one sock placed perpendicular to the top of the other. Got that? Then you fold the toe of the underneath sock over the top sock, then the top sock back over that and so on, tucking the ends into the square. You should finish with a nice folded square, which you can then pop in your sock drawer with all of the others!

- If you are travelling, rolling rather than folding will keep your clothes crease free.

- If you don't have a wardrobe, you might have to be a bit more creative when it comes to storage, but there are plenty of solutions. I don't really like those rails with clothes hanging on them for all to see –

I think they can look very untidy – unless you have some lovely clothes that can be displayed, or are prepared to keep your clothes rail immaculate. The good thing about clothes rails, however, is that they are cheap, so they are ideal if expense is an issue.

- Under the bed is one wardrobe alternative, like those pull-out boxes on wheels; many bed frames come with storage – such as roomy drawers or a unit at the foot of the bed with storage in it – so make full use of these. Some mattresses even lift to reveal clever under-bed storage. Alternatively, you can use bed risers, which look like upside-down flower pots and can be placed under your bed legs to raise the bed for extra storage space. Get help with this – we don't want the bed falling down on you! And take a good look at what you are putting under the bed: make sure that you're not just moving clutter around the house, but really need to store things there.

- Don't forget simple storage things like vacuum bags for your winter duvets. You can place your duvets in them and suck the air out with a vacuum cleaner – it will take up a fraction of the space. This can be done for sleeping bags, cushions, pillows, blankets – meaning more room for your clothes! Make sure that everything you put into these bags is dry!

- Clear plastic boxes will allow you to see what's inside them – ideal if you have a lot of clothes to store, but not all day to look after them. And they are sealed, so no damp or moths!

PAPER TRAIL

Who said that the paperless age would reduce the mountain of paper in our lives? I have moved to paperless billing for utilities, bank statements and the like, but I still come home from my travels or work and find a new mountain of paper in my hall. From junk mail to all those lovely Sunday supplements, it's impossible to escape. But don't be tempted to just throw it all into a heap and forget about it. Organise your paper mountain regularly, before it turns into Everest!

First, invest in a little set of filing drawers for your household bills and correspondence. These can be open or closed – open means that you are unlikely to miss the important bit of correspondence you are supposed to be dealing with, but closed is tidier. Next, take out the big pile of papers you have shoved in a cupboard and place them on the floor, allocating a space for each area of your life – doctor, car, insurance, bank, energy bills etc. – then place each allocated bundle into a marked drawer, making sure that there is nothing to 'action' first. You will need to keep tax records for five years, so this is one instance where I would recommend attic storage.

You should be left with one – hopefully small – pile of paper. Pop an 'in tray' on top of your filing cabinet for things that actually need to be done.

The Noguchi filing system is another method for filing your precious papers. When I read up on it, I was told that it was so easy, my papers would file themselves. 'How I wish it worked like that!' I said – but it is so simple, I can't believe that someone actually needed to come up with the idea. Thankfully, Noguchi Yukio, a Japanese economist and writer, did. The interesting thing about this filing system is that you don't have to prioritise – I know, it seems to run counter to the way we normally file things, but take a closer look and you'll see that the prioritising does happen – all by itself.

Here goes:

1 Buy a pack of brown A4 envelopes.
2 Cut the top inch or so off each envelope, including the flap.
3 Write what's in the envelope along the right-hand side – say, electricity bills. You can put a little coloured tag on the side if you like for each category: Blue for gas bills, brown for insurance and so on.
4 Pop your envelopes vertically on a shelf – i.e. with the open bit at the top – in any order you like. No need to prioritise or anything else.

As you have use for each item, take the envelope down and, when putting it back, place it to the far left of your space. As you go along, you'll notice that the envelopes you use the most are on the left – so you'll always know where they are. Less frequent use will come in the middle and those on the far right – well, after a while you'll know that they are rarely used and that you can put them away somewhere safe. I think it's brilliant and I plan to use it all the time from now on. Simplicity really is the best thing!

TOY STORAGE

When Cathy's children were small, I know that she found toy storage a challenge. She bought big plastic crates for the kids' toys, but when the lid was lifted, all you could see was a big tangle of toys. Thankfully, nowadays, these handy plastic boxes come with in-built dividers, so that you can pop, say, all the toy cars in one bit and all of the figurines in another. You can also get plastic storage units that come with a number of drawers, ideal for things like Lego, which is the bane of every parent's life, I hear! I know that some parents store their children's Lego in ziplock bags, each with the name of the set labelled on it. This is fantastic if you are well organised or have the time to do so – and you don't have a child that likes to mix everything up!

If time is at a premium, a unit with a number of drawers could be just the ticket. You can get cabinets with up to 50 drawers in them, which is ideal if you have lots of little things to store. Drawers are also easier than lids for little fingers to prise open – better still, when your children are small, keep their toys in open plastic buckets: they are easier for you to manage and to encourage your child to put things into when he or she has finished playing with them. I was very taken by the idea of a drawstring play mat: it folds out to be a large play mat, ideal for all kinds of playing, and when your child is finished, you simply pile all of the toys onto the mat, pull the string and haul everything away – great if you are visiting a friend. You can even make one yourself, using sturdy fabric, around which you sew a loose hem, threading some elastic through it. (If you attach a safety pin to your elastic, you can push it along through the material.) I saw one in my travels that had been crocheted by hand, which looked lovely – I can only imagine how long it took to make!

I can see the logic of soft toy 'bins', but I think that they could lead to stockpiling of cuddly animals, which isn't ideal, as they do attract dust. It reminds me of the story a friend of mine told me, about coming into her toddler's bedroom one morning, to find no sign of him. After a panicky few minutes looking around, she discovered him fast asleep in the cuddly toy bin! I can imagine it would have been lovely and comfortable.

Another brilliant tip that I discovered in my research is *not* to buy child-sized storage or shelving. It makes sense, doesn't it? You can't store a lot in teeny-weeny units and you will need storage that grows as your child does. It's more sensible to buy full-size shelving. Buy shelves that can be taken out and moved around to accommodate different-sized toys, and keep the things your child uses most down low.

I did see one 'solution' that advocated colour-coding children's books and using them decoratively. This sounds good in principle – children's books are so lovely to look at nowadays – but can be more difficult if your child wants to take books down to read and puts them back in the 'wrong' place. And imagine the stress of keeping that colour-coded bookshelf colour-coded? Children can be pretty hard on books, so I imagine they would get grubby and stained pretty quickly (the books, that is!).

More useful, and in fact very clever, was the idea of turning one of those chunky white bookcases that you often see in home stores on its side and using it to store toys, books, shoes and art stuff in a child's bedroom – what a good idea!

If space is an issue, or even if it's not, it pays to buy multi-purpose furniture for children: a bed that has storage underneath, a chair that doubles as a box for toy storage, an ottoman that makes a comfy seat and can conceal a multitude underneath.

HOW TO ... SAVE MORE SPACE

Insert a little rack on legs into your kitchen cupboard to store extra tins and jars, and a rail into your under-sink cupboard for bottles of spray cleaner, etc. Tension rods can be very useful here – so you don't even need to get a drill out!

Hang your ironing board on the back of a door, for extra space saving. You can also buy these marvellous clips online that you can push your broom handles into on the back of a door. I have also come across a brilliant folding ironing board that you can pull out from under a kitchen counter. Many terrific space-saving ideas come with modern kitchens – and they don't even have to be expensive.

Drawer dividers don't just help you to keep your socks and underwear under control: they can be used for clips, Post-its, keys, tools, cutlery – in fact, anything that needs to be tidy and easily found.

If your children just throw their dirty clothes on the floor, put a **small laundry hamper** in each bedroom for them – they won't have to throw their clothes a great deal further!

Don't forget things like **magnetic knife strips** – ideal for safety and storage – and for more than just knives. If you have a lot of beauty products like tweezers or eyelash-curlers, with metal parts, or hair grips – a magnetic strip will keep them together. Also, spice jars with magnetic lids are terrific – no need to rummage in the back of the cupboard for the ginger any more.

I have seen very clever uses for **wine racks**, particularly decorative ones, for more than just bottles of wine. Towels, letters, pairs of shoes ... anything that you need to slot into a little niche.

You can 'repurpose' a **paper towel holder** – the type with a little dowel that fits into a base – by sliding bangles or hair ties onto it.

Those **wire-mesh or plastic folder holders** can hold lots of things, from rolls of clingfilm and tin foil to purses and clutch bags.

Plastic pocket holders are great for shoes, but for everything else too, because you can see what you are looking for immediately. You can pin one on the inside of your cupboards to store everything from sponges to small packets of spices or herbs.

PHOTO STORAGE AND PRINTING

My mother had a shelf in the kitchen which served as an in-tray of sorts, where she'd keep bills and that kind of thing that had come in the post. In those days, it was normal for people to get pictures taken at dress dances and to send them to friends, so Mum would also put the pictures of her friends and family in their suits and lovely dresses on the shelf, before filing them away later in 'the box', as we used to call it. On a wet day, when we were very small children, we'd be allowed to open the box and look at all the photos of granny and grandad and all of our relatives – it would keep us occupied for hours. We must have looked at the contents of that box thousands of times!

Recently, my nephew spent a morning downloading pictures from my computer to a 500-GB drive for me – a long way from 'the box'! With photos so easy to take on our phones – and so easy to see – it's tempting to leave digital as well as real clutter behind us.

If you have lots of 'real' photos, spend one morning putting them into frames that you've bought cheaply from the DIY or furniture store – or better still, delegate the job to one of the children.

You can also go to any one of the many services online that will print photos for you or make them into a calendar. This can be lovely if you have holiday photos you want to remember, or, as a friend of mine did, a monthly photo of her dog! Another friend got a number of family photos enlarged and mounted onto an art board, which looked lovely and modern with no frames needed, and you can also get photos mounted on other surfaces too, including metal and canvas.

I don't like albums, because they take up so much of our precious space and because they can make the photos fade, but I love to see photos in frames. I think that some of the nicest frames can be ones that children have made in school – they are often part of an art project – and putting a photo in one reminds you of your child as well as of the photo itself.

Be careful when storing photos – the attic or the basement is not the place; the attic can be too warm and dry, the basement too cold and damp, and both could result in damaged photos. Get a separate box for the negatives – again, store these carefully so that they don't get damaged. If a photo is particularly precious, consider having it scanned, so that you can store it digitally. And don't store your photos in any old box – buy a box that is designed to store photographs. Filtered glass will stop your photos fading, but don't put them on a bright sunny wall, as they will fade so quickly.

'Cloud' storage is perfect for uploading and sharing photos with family members. It's also private, so the world doesn't have to see them. However, many services aren't free, and what they offer does vary. Some services won't let people upload photos from, say, their Facebook account, which I can imagine would be trying for younger people; other services sound like fun for this age group, allowing you to add special effects and doodles to your photos – it's not for me, but again, young people will probably cheer. What I like is to know that my photos are safe, so I want photos that I take on my phone to be uploaded to the cloud (don't I sound modern!) and saved there, so I can get them whenever I want. If you are a keen photographer, you can get an app for your phone that will auto-upload your photos, which will free up space on your camera roll.

HOW TO ... AVOID CABLE CHAOS

As we know, charging cables for TVs, computers and mobile phones can get into a terrible mess, but thankfully there are lots of products nowadays that will help you to keep them in order. First, though – throw out any old chargers that no longer work or belong to a phone you bought 10 years ago! Now you can streamline your charging cables by **buying a cable sleeve**, through which you thread all of your cables to keep them tidy, or a series of clips into which you push your cables to keep them separate – great for a desk. You can fit your cables and clips into a sleek black or white box, which can be purchased at computer stores and online, if you like things to look nice.

You can also buy a **single cable with multiple connectors** on it: a connector for USBs, mobile phones, iPhones, iPads etc. This will reduce the number of cables, and you won't need to pick up yet another cable and wonder what it's for. You can also find 'charging hubs' at your computer store or online that will allow you to plug in a number of USBs or devices in one place. If cable mess is getting you down, you could also try a 'cable yoyo' – it's pretty much as it sounds: a circular 'yoyo' device with a single USB key attached, around which you wrap your cables, plugging the USB into a port. A great idea! I found one in one of the many gadget shops now springing up.

If you have pets that nibble cables – and some do – try **cable 'wrap'**, a grey spiral into which you thread your cables. It's tough enough to withstand most little teeth.

Many newer plugs and even wall sockets now come with **handy slots for USB** and mobile phone cables too. If you can't find them, you will be able to find wall chargers that will have one attachment for the wall, and in it, many different slots for your various devices.

If you don't have an immediate use for your cable, store it away in a **handy cable storage pocket**, along with your USB keys and those phone earbuds that keep disappearing! You can buy travel cases, too, that have pockets for wires, USB keys, charging ports etc.

Speaking of earbuds, they can also get into a terrible tangle. I like those **plastic gadgets in the shape of a fish skeleton** for wrapping your earphone cables around; other ideas include a 'doggie' earphone organiser (I detect an animal theme here!) – you can place your earbuds into Fido's ears ...

CHAPTER THREE

Your Cosy Home – Furniture, Interiors and Other Lovely Things

◇◇◇◇◇◇◇◇◇◇◇◇◇◇◇◇◇◇◇◇◇◇◇◇◇◇◇◇◇◇

*'Forget grandeur – I don't think it's a
quality we want today.'*

ALBERT HADLEY

When I was young, we had a 'good room', where none of us was allowed to set foot. It was always immaculate, with a lovely china cabinet and the best sofa, with antimacassars draped over the back of it. (They were called that because they prevented hair oil or Macassar oil from staining the sofa fabric.) The good room was for guest use only, and when the parish priest would call, he would be ushered in to sit beside the fire.

Nowadays we use every room in the house and guests can take us as we are. We also lead completely different lives from our forebears. We work outside the home for long hours, men and women share household tasks, we have blended families with children coming and going, and we have less and less time to be at home. Which makes our homes all the more important as havens, places where we can relax and be ourselves. It's also true to say that we just don't have the same amount of time as in previous generations, so housekeeping and looking after the home has to be simple and fuss-free. No one wants to come home from a long day at the office to polish the silver!

Our homes need to be clean and comfortable – but they don't have to be fussy or grand. You don't have to be an interiors expert to want to create a warm, welcoming home – nor do you have to have a lot of money. Simple tips will make your home its very best, without costing you a fortune. Consider what really matters to you in a home. Some of us suffer from home envy, and a sense of wanting to 'keep up with the Joneses'. We want that lovely conservatory that Mr and Mrs O'Reilly have had specially designed – but think about it: conservatories are baking in summer and freezing in winter, so possibly not the best use of precious space for, say, busy families. Perhaps you yearn for a separate dining room, with a lovely table and matching chairs, but do you want to spend all of your time lugging dishes in and out of the kitchen, or do you want to sit in there, eating, wondering what the kids are up to in the living room? What about open-plan space? It's so nice when the children are small, but do you want teenagers and their friends sitting on top of you, roaring at the Playstation when you're trying to read the paper? What about playrooms

– they tend to be repositories for junk, as I'm reliably informed! Some people think that they won't be happy unless they have an en suite for every bedroom – but that's an awful lot of bathrooms to clean!

Of course, many of us don't have the luxury of being able to make these choices, because perhaps we live in a period home, with lots of small rooms, or in an apartment or a cottage; maybe we live in a new-build that has a pre-designed layout. One thing is certain: increasingly, space is at a premium for many of us, so that's another decision we have to make – how to make the most of limited space.

So let's start with some space-saving tips for your homes, to bring everything up to the 21st century!

FINDING SPACE

The first thing when it comes to space is to make the most of hidden or wasted space – under the stairs, recesses in walls, around beds, under beds; above and underneath appliances. You'd be surprised where you can find space once you start to look.

Under the stairs is one of the easiest places to find that extra space, whether it's for an extra toilet, a home office or a series of pull-out drawers for all the stuff that normally gets thrown in the hall, like bags, coats, footballs etc. While I was doing my research, I saw a lovely bookcase built under the stairs in an interiors magazine, which looked very smart – now I know what to do with all of my coffee-table books. I also came across a nice little bench seat with storage underneath, where you could hide away for a bit, and where you can store shoes, wellies, raincoats, that kind of thing. I also came across a dog house that someone had lovingly built under their stairs, complete with porthole for doggy to look into the garden. At least it keeps the rest of the home clean and doggy free!

If space is tight, under the stairs can be a good spot for a home office, if you don't need absolute silence in which to work. If the idea of converting your stairs brings you out in a rash, there are now any number of companies that will fit under-stairs storage for you – at a price. Under the stairs is a tricky area, so it's hard to do yourself unless you really are handy. If you're not, you could put something simple but useful there, like a bureau, in which you keep correspondence, bills, book lists etc., or a simple bench with under-storage for shoes, brollies and sports equipment.

Built-in cabinets used to be considered a bit dated, and in fact, lots of people ripped them out when they were refurbishing their homes, but cabinets have come a long way and are great if you want to really use the space above appliances, or above the bed. Another handy and pretty option in bedrooms is a daybed – part sofa, part bed – that has a nice frame and comes with the option of storage or a pull-out bed underneath.

In the bathroom, my favourite storage example was underneath the bath! Clever panels pulled back to reveal little racks with shampoo bottles and sponges – very resourceful. The only drawback, again, is that built-in solutions are hard to do yourself. If you are lucky enough to be re-doing your bathroom, you can install 'floating' loos and sinks that are fixed to hidden units in the wall, rather than having a pedestal. This will give you valuable space underneath, as well as creating the illusion of having more space.

When it comes to saving space in the *living room*, don't forget the humble sofa bed – I even came across one in the course of my research that folded into bunk beds, which was most impressive, but perhaps not for all types of guest! A bracket for wall mounting your TV set will also free up space underneath for more storage. Shelving in living rooms is a must, and you can buy units that have open shelves and cupboards to display your nice things and store your not-so-nice things!

If your sitting room is small, don't install a great big leather sofa in it: find a sofa that's neat – how about vintage? Sofas and chairs from the 1950s and 1960s were smaller and neater and a chaise longue could be very stylish, as well as being neat and tidy. A daybed might even work in a living room, because some of the modern ones are very stylish and tidy and, of course, double as a bed for guests.

If you must have a coffee table, pick a small one that you can pop beside the sofa, with storage underneath for magazines and papers, or a trunk or chest that doubles as a coffee table.

Mirrors are excellent for creating a sense of space, and if you are brave, you could do away with a rug and leave just a plain carpet or boards – again, you'll create the illusion that the space is bigger than it is. Another handy trick for fooling the eye is to hang your curtains from a point just below the ceiling, rather than from your window – which will make your room look taller.

Kitchens come nowadays with all kinds of handy storage units, from pot drawers in a handy corner unit, to a slimline pull-out drawer for condiments beside the cooker. If you don't want to go for a complete kitchen refurbishment just to get rid of the clutter, any home or DIY store will have a selection of racks, jars, magnetic strips and that kind of thing to help you to tidy up your kitchen cupboards. Here are my favourite kitchen storage ideas:

- **The top of the cupboards – that foot or so between the top of the cupboard and the ceiling that normally just collects dust – can be a great place for storage. A row of baskets for all the things that we normally shove in a drawer would be just the thing – lightbulbs, spare batteries, instruction manuals for kitchen equipment, the bowl that is only used for Christmas pudding – that kind of thing. Make sure it's something you don't want to use every day, or you'll get an awful lot of exercise! I'd be wary of using this space for nice things, like ornaments, as you'll have to take them down to dust them quite often, and they'll also get covered in a layer of grease. Extra storage for wine, though, is an idea, or extra storage jars for your annual jam-making.**

- Kitchen drawers nowadays come with lots of handy storage ideas built into them; those narrow drawers that pull out beside the cooker are great for storing – well, narrow things! They are actually designed to take bottles, but you could also use them for the utensils that you use every day, on a row of hooks, or tall pasta jars.

- You can get a knife block set into a drawer – handy if you are a keen cook with a nice knife collection – but make sure that the drawer is out of the reach of little fingers. You could even get a deep drawer with the square bin dividers in them for storing something other than rubbish – say, dry ingredients. During my research, I also saw a pull-out drawer just beneath the counter that had room for a digital scales, which is very handy. And if a bespoke kitchen drawer is more than you can afford, remember, many drawer insets can be bought cheaply nowadays from DIY stores – but think first about what you use most in your kitchen. If you're a master baker, you won't want to hunt around for jars and packets in every cupboard; if you're a cook, you will want your spice collection readily available, or if you like juicing, you might want to buy a nice deep drawer divider for all the juicer's components.

- If you don't have room for a pot drawer, a handy alternative is to hang them over the cooker or, if you'd prefer, to get some hooks screwed – firmly! – into the end of your last cupboard and hang them there – that way they are tidy as well as handy.

- A final note of warning if you're doing DIY. Don't go digging holes in the walls without checking first to see if there's any wiring or pipes. You can buy a device in the hardware store that will emit a loud 'beep' if wires are near. (You can tell that I don't do a lot of DIY!)

SOFAS AND COVERS

A friend of mine spent a fortune on a new sofa not so long ago … a good idea in my book. The sofa is the one thing I feel that you shouldn't skimp on, if you can. A good sofa will last you a lifetime. But what did she discover when she took it home? That the covers were dry-clean only! Not a bother, she thought – she'd just whip them off every so often and take them to the dry-cleaners, but honestly, she was driven mad with them. She has a busy home, a family and pets, so you can imagine how dirty the lovely cream sofa got and how quickly. In the end, she opted to hand wash the covers, only to find that she had to squeeze the cushions a bit too tightly back into the covers and they now have a very 'stretched' look about them. I know now, after all my research, that you need to put sofa covers back on when they are still very slightly damp, so that they'll stretch, but it's too late for my friend!

If a really good sofa is going to be one of the major items of expenditure in your home, it pays to make sure that the covering is sturdy and easy to maintain. You can actually remove a lot of general dirt with your hoover, and can loosen other stains with a brush – a lint roller works wonders removing pet hair, by the way, as many people find that it clogs up the vacuum.

I'm a big fan of washable covers, as they really are the easiest option, but be careful when you do wash them to follow the instructions on the care label. Generally these will be for a cool wash – but, of course, you'll find that the toughest stains won't come out. Pre-treat the toughest stains with a fabric shampoo – don't use anything that will bleach out the stain – and then wash them on a cool setting. Beware though: don't wash them too often or they'll end up a different colour from the cover of the sofa back itself. I have a lovely pair of arm savers that are two shades lighter than my sofa for that very reason!

Sadly, sofa covers do have a habit of shrinking, unless they are 'pre-shrunk'. If in doubt, it pays to test out a little bit of fabric first. Dampen a bit of the fabric on your sofa, say, on one of the arm savers; if it puckers don't wash the rest. The same goes for the colour running. Dampen a bit of fabric first and press a bit of white kitchen paper against it – if the colour runs onto the paper – be safe and take it to the dry cleaners.

If your sofa has 'fixed' covers, you won't be able to wash them. Instead – *and only if your fixed covers are washable* – you'll need to use a steam cleaner or carpet shampooer to do the job. I think you'll need a little man for this, but if you want to tackle the job yourself, you can hire a specialist shampooer – follow the instructions to avoid disaster! The same rules for loose covers also apply to fixed – soggy fabric has a habit of shrinking, and you don't want the board underneath to get wet under any circumstances, so don't overdo it. Use foam, not water, and dry the fabric as quickly as possible. However, if you want your sofa to last for ever, this is one area where I'd recommend professional cleaning. It might seem expensive, but it's cheaper than replacing a water-damaged sofa.

Many people feel that leather is a more durable alternative to fabric, and it certainly is robust, but stains can damage it, as can bright sunlight. Only use a specialist leather cleaner on your lovely sofa; if it stains, don't go at it with a harsh cleaner. A damp cloth is enough for daily use, and a very gentle solution of diluted soap flakes, like Lux, or a dab of a mild soap, like Dove or Ivory, will also work on a stain – but don't soak the leather. Another handy cleaner is a mixture of equal parts water and vinegar. Dab onto a soft cloth, then wipe the sofa with it – do not soak the cloth!

If you want to avoid any potential sofa-cover disasters, follow these handy tips:

- **No eating on the sofa. My mother would have died if we'd eaten anywhere else but at the table, but nowadays, snacking is the done thing. If you must snack, don't do so on the sofa.**

- **Vacuum your sofa gently but thoroughly often, to remove crumbs – if someone has sneakily eaten!**

- **Don't put your sofa in the living room window, or the fabric colour will fade very quickly.**

If you want to remove stains from fabric sofas with washable covers:

- **Treat them as soon as you see them.**

- Apply a dab of warm water mixed with a drop of washing-up liquid to blot the stain. Don't rub it, or it will sink into the fabric. Dry with a paper towel and leave.

- Zap the stain with steam from your iron to see if you can loosen it.

- Cornflour or bicarbonate of soda sprinkled onto grease stains and left for half an hour before being vacuumed away might be just the job.

- Soda water can help to remove wine or coffee stains, because the bubbles 'lift' some of the stain with them, so pour a little on your red wine stain before you blot it with a paper towel. Salt is also effective. Get to the stain quickly, douse it in plenty of salt and leave a while for the salt to absorb before vacuuming. It won't have disappeared, but you'll have less of a stain to work on with either a specialist stain-remover or a solution of water mixed with washing-up liquid.

- On pale leather, a paste of equal parts lemon juice and cream of tartar can help with stain removal. Don't use this for general cleaning though, and always, always spot check, before letting loose with any cleaner.

CUSHIONS AND THROWS

Throws come into their own if you have pets or children. It's hard to keep either of them off the sofa, I'm told, so if your Labrador will insist on living on the sofa, use a washable throw. Throws can also be used to save your sofa from sticky fingers, crayon marks or other spills and to brighten a drab or tired sofa fabric. Throws can also look lovely folded at the end of a bed or for wrapping around yourself if you get chilly. Some people think they are a bit fussy, but if you keep it simple and don't use them absolutely everywhere, they can look lovely. Some people are fond of great big furry throws, but not me! I like them simple and neat – and I don't like the fashion for flinging them casually over the back of the sofa either. I like them to be folded neatly behind the sofa cushions, which I've picked in a contrasting colour, so the whole thing looks tidy.

Throws don't have to be just functional – pay attention to colour, texture and pattern when you are buying. If you have a cream sofa, try a shot of orange or vivid blue to brighten it. Keep crazy patterns and bold florals for the bedroom, where you won't frighten the visitors!

Cushions aren't essential (some people hate them) but they make things look nice and can dress up furniture – imagine a bare sofa, without any cushions on it – it would look quite spartan. It's true that cushions can be a bit of an affectation these days. My mother only used a few velvet-covered stiff cushions on the sofa and she would never have dreamt of putting cushions on a bed, but I think that cushions make a room look that bit more special, even a bedroom, particularly if they contrast with the bedclothes or with the nice throw draped across the end of the bed.

Whenever I think of cushions, I'm reminded of my Granny's chair. This lovely comfortable chair had been sitting near the open fire in the old family home in Sligo for many years when my brother Damien got a notion to re-upholster it. He set to, removing the old cushion pads, and what should he discover only a hidden cache of bullets. They had clearly been there for a long time, because they were made of brass, but how Granny hadn't gone up in a puff of smoke, sitting beside the open fire, I'll never know! Being upstanding citizens, we brought the bullets to the Gardaí, who examined them carefully and declared that they were probably from the Civil War.

When it comes to cushions, I'm not a fan of matchy-matchy. I like my cushions to be nice and firm and to be in a contrasting colour or pattern to my sofa. I know that maybe cousin Joan has brought you back a nice cushion cover from Rhodes with a picture of a fishing boat on it – it's lovely, I'm sure, but you can use it in the bedroom or the guest room. Cushions in the living room should pull together or lift your colour scheme, drawing from the colour of, say, a painting above the fireplace or some other colour that you've used in the room. It doesn't have to match it, but it does have to echo it – don't pick colours that you don't have in your living room or your cushions will clash with everything else.

Decide whether you want your sofa to look like it's from a hotel, with lots of neatly arranged cushions, or from a family home, where you have a more haphazard arrangement. If you have a family, the cushions will get thrown around, and if you have a pet, you might want to lift them before Fido decides he'd like to rest his head on them!

Try to vary the shapes of your cushions – unless you prefer a very tidy look – by choosing different sizes or mixing square and bolster shapes. When it comes to arranging your cushions, you could put a large one at the back and a smaller one in front, right in the middle of your sofa cushion, for a very geometric look; or you could arrange them in a row, it really depends on the shape of your cushions, but working from the outside into the middle of the sofa with your cushions is a good rule of thumb.

CATHY'S TIP

If you are plumping your cushions, don't bash them in the middle. Pick the cushion up by the top right-hand corner and by the bottom left and tug gently into position.

Some people like a very 'overstuffed' look with two rows of cushions with different patterns for a very eclectic look. This is a bit of a nightmare for me, because I like things to look tidy, but I can see the appeal for modern families, when the cushions will probably get thrown around a bit. One thing, though – unless you have allergies, buy feathers if you can afford them, rather than foam for the inside. Feathers give cushions a lovely squishy feel – and a more expensive one too! Posh cushions can be a way of lifting a cheaper sofa or bed, or adding some colour to a drab room, so they are worth the investment. And, if you are handy (or even if you're not), they are easy to make. The simple instructions below will help you to make an 'envelope' cushion – that is, one that has an opening at the back, like the flap of an envelope. Easy-peasy, because you don't have to sew in a zip. You could do the sewing by hand, but I'd recommend a machine, because the stitching won't come undone.

- Buy your cushion pad first, from a home store – cushion pads normally come in a range of sizes, like 46cm x 33cm, and with different fillings, from synthetic to duck feather. Duck feather is lovely, but not for allergy sufferers!

- The front piece of your fabric will need to be about 3cm larger than your padding all the way around. This is important, so that your pad will fit in and you'll have room for a hem. The back piece will need to be the same size as your front bit, but with an extra 8cm, because this will be the flap of your envelope shape.

- Cut your back piece – the larger piece, in two equal halves. You'll need to hem the inner edge of each piece, folding and pinning the hem on the wrong side of the fabric, and then sewing in a straight line all the way along. Now you have your two seams for the envelope part done.

- Line up your front piece – the full square – with the two back pieces. You place the square, patterned side down, on a flat surface, then line up the first smaller piece – unsewn edge to unsewn edge – patterned side down again. Next, line up the next small piece in the same way, against the unsewn outer edge of the square – you'll have an overlap of fabric – your envelope.

- Pin your cushion all the way around, then sew all the way around, about a half a centimetre in from the edge.

- If you want to avoid puckered corners, snip the fabric at each corner – above the stitching – at an angle.

- Turn your cover inside out – pop your cushion pad in – and you're done!

CURTAINS AND BLINDS

Curtains used to be big, heavy old things in velvet, with lining and a pelmet. There was a reason for this, of course: to keep drafts out of our chilly homes, long before central heating! Now, with our passive houses and new-builds, they aren't even needed – at least for draught exclusion. Curtains can simply be decorative or for privacy – and some people have done away with them altogether in favour of blinds or even shutters. We're also more aware of things like allergies nowadays, so many of us avoid dust-collecting curtains.

If you do have curtains, caring for them properly is important. Vacuum them regularly, so that they don't hang on to dust, using the soft-brush bit of your vacuum cleaner; air them regularly, because they can hold smells – take them outside and hang them in the fresh air. If you need to wash them, be sure to follow the fabric-care instructions: some fabrics are fine to go in the washing machine, but beware of shrinking. If you're in doubt, hand-wash them, using a detergent suitable for delicates. If your curtain fabrics are delicate or have a particular finish – don't throw them in the wash. Dry cleaning (if you really need to – airing and vacuuming might be enough) is safest. If mould is a problem – as it often can be in Ireland, add a cupful of vinegar to your wash.

Steam-cleaning is a good option for curtains that can't be easily washed or taken down. Make sure, though, that you are steam-cleaning them, not soaking them! You don't need to wet the curtain, so hold the cleaner a good 30cm away from the curtains. Follow the steam-cleaner instructions carefully and don't burn yourself!

For those of you who have net curtains, either baking soda or vinegar will help. Pop your nets into a suitable container and then add water, to which you have added 250ml of vinegar or 250g of baking soda. Vinegar is great for whiteness, baking soda good for smells. Do not use both together! If your nets are antiques, be careful: vinegar is great for synthetic fabrics, but too harsh for anything with linen or wool. If in any doubt, hand-wash your nets, but more modern nets can be put on a delicate cycle in the washing machine and you can add some vinegar to the rinse cycle for extra brightness, unless your fabric contains linen.

Venetian blinds used to be all the rage in the 1970s, but now they are often replaced by roller blinds, because Venetians can be fiddly to keep clean. You can use your duster attachment on your hoover to – gently – lift dust, and every so often, a solution of diluted washing-up liquid can be wiped over the blinds to keep them clean. With wooden blinds, don't use water! Just close them so that the slats are all facing the same direction and dust them. Warm, soapy water is best for Venetian blinds.

For all of these blinds, you can also get one of those funny-looking blind cleaners in the DIY store. They look like the fingers of a hand, with little dust pads on each finger, attached to a little plastic handle and are very effective for cleaning a number of individual slats.

As for Roman blinds ... well, I'm not a fan! They look lovely, but only if they hang right – and they never hang right! They are also great dust collectors, so not ideal for people with allergies and they are hard to clean yourself. You'll need to get the professionals in. I rest my case! I really like shutters, however, because they are easy to clean and maintain, and they look nice, but for easy care, my favourites are roller blinds. They come in so many different colours and patterns nowadays and the fabrics used are often so easy to clean – just a wipe with a damp cloth will do it.

If your blinds are really grubby, you can give them a bath in mild detergent and a gentle rub with a sponge – but do check first to make sure that the fabric can be soaked in water.

Of course, I must mention fire safety with all upholstered products! Furnishings made after 1990 have to have a label on them that declares that they have passed stringent fire-safety tests, but this does not apply to furniture made before 1950, so be aware if you like retro pieces. Check for fire-safety labels when you buy second-hand furniture – businesses that deal in second-hand furniture are obliged to check that it carries the appropriate label.

PAINTS AND WALLPAPER

Of course, the Chinese were the first to invent paper – as they were to invent so many things – as far back as the first century AD, but they didn't use decorative wallpaper in their own homes, it seems. Instead, they began to export patterned paper to Europe in the 17th century. Early wallpaper was painted onto silk as well as paper, which must have been gorgeous – and a change from the kind of tapestries that had adorned the walls in better-off homes at the time. Of course, wallpaper was for the wealthy, having been brought back on ships by companies like the East India Company, but Oliver Cromwell soon put paid to that. In his view, wallpaper was frivolous and so he banned it! When wallpaper returned, new processes meant that it became increasingly used by the middle classes, and panoramic scenes were very popular, with each wallpaper panel telling part of a visual 'story' – what a nice idea. It was only in the 19th century, however, with cheap printing presses, that wallpaper began to be mass produced and available to the less wealthy. I can imagine that it would have brightened dark, gloomy rooms at the time. Of wallpaper designers at the time, William Morris is probably the best known for his lovely Arts and Crafts designs. Now, digital printing has made a lot of new techniques possible, including wallpaper that has LED lighting in it! My dad would have loved that, because he was a great wallpaperer. He'd get the plumb line and start in the corner. He did try to teach me, but I never got the hang of it!

Wallpaper has always been a practical choice for many, because it covers a multitude, and in some older homes, peeling back wallpaper reveals layer upon layer of earlier papers. It's like interior archaeology. Now, wallpapers come in every conceivable pattern and texture, and in a variety of finishes. Unfortunately, they haven't yet worked out how to make it hang itself, but I'm sure that'll happen!

Vinyl wallpaper is probably the one that most of us use, because it's practical, being washable; then there's fabric-backed vinyl, which is extra tough and good for playrooms and hallways.

Foil wallpapers are very pretty, with their lovely silvery sheens and nice finishes, but they can be difficult to hang and you need to be careful to cover dents and holes in the wall before hanging. If you have an uneven wall or one with a bright paint colour, you might need to use a lining paper first. Check with your DIY shop if in doubt – and lining paper is hung in the opposite direction to the wallpaper that will cover it, in case you didn't know. One thing about foil papers is that they repel moisture, so you could use one in your bathroom if you fancied an opulent finish.

I will gloss over wood-chip paper, because it is a bit dated nowadays and so on to *anaglypta* paper, which is a very posh name for plain, embossed wallpaper. Apparently, it was all the range in the late 19th century and it has a touch of the institutional about it, but it's very useful if you have uneven walls that you want to hide. Many people paint over the paper, too, and treat it with all kinds of finishes, which can really give it a modern look.

Flock wallpaper might send a shiver down your spine – it always reminds me of old pubs – but nowadays, flock patterns can actually be very nice and come in very modern patterns, and if you really want 'bespoke', you can order a hand-printed wallpaper, with anything from modern patterns to the revival of historic ones, from the Georgian and Victorian eras. Lovely, but expensive!

When you buy your rolls of wallpaper, you'll see little symbols on the label, which will tell you whether it's washable, and how it might fade in bright sunlight, as well as whether you need to paste the wall, the paper, or whether the paper comes pre-pasted, which is handy. Your label may also include information about how to hang the pattern, so that it matches. If money isn't an issue, you can get a specialist to hang your wallpaper for you, but if you are on a budget, here is a little checklist.

- Once you've decided on your pattern, you'll need to calculate how many rolls of paper you'll need. UK wallpaper sizes can be a little bit bigger than European ones, so check what size your roll is and check what size the pattern is: the larger the pattern, the more leftovers you'll have.

- Then, measure the perimeter of your room – that is, the measurement of each wall, added together. Say you have two walls of three meters and two walls of two meters, then the perimeter is 10 meters. Then you need to look at the height of the walls. Include any extras, like corners – where you'll use more paper – and fireplaces, doorways etc. If in doubt, your local DIY store will help you to calculate, as will many online wallpaper/DIY websites.

- You'll need to prepare the walls first, by making sure that there are no holes or bumps in the plasterwork, but if you intend to fit, say, supports for shelves, and have drilled holes in the wall for them, pop a matchstick in the holes and when you roll out the paper, press the matchstick through the paper to indicate where you'll be placing screws.

- Measure the length of the wall from top to bottom and cut your paper a few inches longer, to allow for trimming. You'll need to pay careful attention to the pattern in the wallpaper as you go, to make sure it lines up. Cut all of the lengths of paper you'll be needing for one wall at a time, and leave them ready – this will help you to assess how the pattern matches up.

- Of course, there are many commercial pastes now, instead of the old flour-and-water mix that we all used to use, so check which paste you'll need and how to mix it.

- Mixing wallpaper paste is a bit like cutting hair: too much water and you'll be left with a runny paste that's hard to fix; too little water and you can thin it as needed. You'll probably need to let it stand for a little while before using.

- If you have a pasting table, great, but most people won't, so you can use an old door or a table – but make sure it isn't so wide that you have to run back and forth while pasting! You need to be able to do it in a sweep.

- When you have pasted your paper, fold it into accordion pleats and let the paste settle into the paper for about 10 to 15 minutes.

- **You'll need to draw a 'plumb line' for your paper, because very few walls are dead straight, and hang from this line. Begin near a window and around you go. If you want to avoid wonky patterns, centre the pattern on a fireplace or central feature of your room.**

- **Keep paste only on the back of the wallpaper – if any gets on the front, wipe it off with a sponge. And make sure to keep your tools clean and dry so that you don't end up in a big mess!**

- **If you have any pattern mismatch, make sure that it's above or below eye level, where it is less likely to be noticed.**

Paints might seem like a much simpler option after the challenges of wallpaper hanging, and they are certainly easier to apply – if not as good at covering imperfections. Paints used to be oil-based, and take ages to dry – maybe that's where the expression 'watching paint dry' comes from! – as well as having terrible fumes. Nowadays, most paints are water-based, also called 'latex', so they dry more quickly and are less smelly, but they are less hard-wearing and you might need to apply more coats to get the same effect. You might find that you use an oil-based paint for your skirting boards, because they will get a lot of wear, or the lintel in the doorway, and then water-based for the walls.

The subject of paint reminds me of our handyman. Every home had one in those days, because appliances were designed to be repaired, and because there were always 'little jobs' to do around the house. Anyway, we were only delighted to find this man, because he also worked for a well-to-do family in the area, so he had to be good! Mum asked him to paint the front door to match our 'grained' front facade of the house. I'm not sure if any of you recall 'graining', but it was a technique where yellow plaster was applied to the front of the house and large combs were pulled through it in a swirly pattern. It was all the rage way back when! Anyway, our handyman was to paint the front door to match, and Mum left him to it, while she went out for the day. When she came back, the house door was an eye-watering shade of bright blue – it was roaring at us! 'What in the name of

God did you do that for?' my mother exclaimed. The man replied, 'What's wrong with it? I had some left over from the other place, and if it's good enough for them, it's good enough for you!'

I'm sure door colours are a lot more tasteful nowadays, and, of course, paints also come in a lot of different finishes, starting with *matte*, which, as it suggests, isn't shiny, but instead has a nice smooth texture and is good at covering up imperfections in walls, but is harder to clean and less easy to use in high-traffic areas like kitchens. Then there's *eggshell*, which unlike its name, is actually more durable than matte and good for kitchens and hallways, and *satin*, which is a bit shinier than eggshell, and which you might use in a bathroom, where you want an easy-clean surface, but not that shiny gloss finish – or if you want to catch light. Eggshell is the best choice if you have walls that aren't the best, as satin shows up more imperfections. And then there's *gloss* itself, which is hard-wearing and good for doors, architraves, skirting boards and so on. You can also get *semi-gloss* nowadays, which is a softer version, but still easy to clean. I've seen it suggested that you can brighten up walls by painting a stripe of gloss paint over a matte wall, or even paint one wall in gloss to pep up your room, if you are really brave.

Whatever finish you decide on, make sure that your wall is prepared first, by cleaning it down and by filling in any holes. Some people use a primer to pre-treat the surface before painting. If you have just bought an old house with ancient paint on the walls, make sure that it doesn't have any lead in it before you try to dust or sand it, scattering nasty particles around.

When it comes to colour, really, your choices are limitless nowadays, but here are a few little guidelines:

- **If you're moving into a new house, you might be tempted to paint the rooms before you move your furniture in. Don't! The paint colour will look completely different when you have your things in it. It might clash with your new sofa or dining table. Wait until you've settled in before you let loose with the paintbrush.**

- Always bring your colour charts home, so that you can see them in the kind of light you have in your home. That way, your colour choice will be truly accurate.

- Painting the walls should be last when you are decorating your home. Think about it. Are you going to buy furniture and bedlinen that matches the colour of your walls, or vice versa?

- With all of the colours available to us, and all of the ranges, it can be overwhelming, so narrow down your options by avoiding a few common mistakes. For instance, black is all the rage as an interior colour at the moment – but think about how it will look on a gloomy Irish December morning! Darker colours might look bold, but they can also make a room seem as if it's closing in on you, if you haven't got lots of natural light.

- A friend of mine painted her kitchen an eye-watering shade of yellow, because she thought it would make it look nice and bright – be careful with colour. It can be tempting to opt for cheery bright colours, but think about actually living with livid red walls or an orange bathroom! If you'd like to try colour, why not paint in a matte finish – it's less lurid than gloss – and paint one wall to make colour 'pop', and not hurt your eyes.

- Paint your samples on your walls not just in little dabs, but in a nice big stripe – and paint on walls that have direct sunlight and walls that don't to get a real idea of colour. Also, think about how your paint colour will look with your flooring.

- A few years ago, we all went mad with 'accent' and 'feature' walls – but these can be hard to get right. If you have a hideous fireplace that you can't afford to change, don't make this your accent wall! Similarly, don't make a feature out of the door that leads to the hall or the stairs. Make it something that you'd like to highlight, like your lovely bay window or your vintage Aga. Many people make a feature out of the wall at the head of their bed, which makes for a nice symmetry and can pull together other colours in the room, like the duvet or cushions. Tiny rooms are not candidates for feature walls, as they can make the space look even tinier – so no accent wall in the downstairs loo!

- On the other hand, don't chicken out and paint everything in magnolia. If you make a mistake with a colour, so what? You can paint over it! Be brave and give more interesting colours a shot. Keep an eye out for interiors magazines or friends' homes that work well.

- White can look fantastic, but it won't brighten a gloomy room – instead, it might make it look a bit grubby and faded. Keep white for lighter spaces.

FLOORS

My mother used to have an Axminster carpet, a rich woollen weave with a patterned swirl in it, of a kind that was very common at the time. Carpets were very expensive, of good quality and staining was the stuff of nightmares! That's probably why we had all of those swirly patterns. I still think that there is nothing better than the cosy feel of a good, thick carpet, even though many people opt for wooden floors nowadays. Wooden floors are certainly easier to clean, particularly if there are allergies in the house, but I prefer carpets in bedrooms, because bedrooms are – or should be! – quiet spaces.

Thankfully you can buy carpets nowadays that are hard wearing and you can buy wool or synthetic carpets. Of course, wool is more expensive, but if you can afford it – and aren't afraid to look after it – it will last longer and look nicer. And the great thing about modern woollen carpets is that they can usually be cleaned without fading or shrinking. Of course, vacuuming regularly will keep your carpet looking good, but some carpet manufacturers caution against using certain types of vacuum, particularly the more vigorous cleaners, as they can damage the carpet fibres. However, you can keep your carpet as good as new if you avoid certain vacuuming 'mistakes'.

It might seem strange to talk about making mistakes with a vacuum, but it's often happened to us in the hotel. We have a bit of a problem with ants, particularly when they start flying, and we do our best to keep them under control. However, one of the girls was vacuuming one day and didn't she vacuum up a whole lot of ants, thinking that she was doing us all a big favour in ridding us of these pests! She left the vacuum cleaner in the store room, and the next day we had about four million ants! They were so delighted at having this cosy, warm place that they bred all night and there were ants everywhere. The moral of the story is – empty the vacuum bag immediately. Also, I always tell all new workers at the hotel when they're vacuuming not to go near the fire if it's on. Why? Because once, one of the girls vacuumed up hot ashes and, not realising her mistake, up she went to the store with the vacuum cleaner and put it neatly away – where it proceeded to smoulder away – there was no fire, thankfully, but there was a ton of smoke.

Here are some common mistakes that people make when vacuuming:

- *Not using all of the attachments.* **You don't need to hold your vacuum up in the air to catch cobwebs – you use the attachment with the angled nozzle. Use the soft brush for dusting or vacuuming upholstery, and the little 'crevice' brush for getting into awkward spots and for vacuuming along the edge of the carpet.**

- *Not emptying the bag or cylinder fully.* **I'm guilty of this sin, I must confess, but if you don't empty your bag, or clear out the cylinder, your vacuum cleaner will not be as effective.**

- *Not cleaning the filter.* **Many vacuum cleaners come with a washable filter – but it does need to be washed, or your cleaner will not work effectively.**

- *Not clearing blockages.* **Hands up those of you who cheerfully vacuum even though you know the brush roll has a covering of pet hair on it? Clean off any hair tangles or you might end up damaging the motor.**

CATHY'S TIP:

Go over your carpets more than once when you are vacuuming, to make sure that things like pet hair are fully removed. Once is not enough when it comes to tricky dirt in carpets.

When it comes to cleaning your carpet, you can get in the professionals or you can hire a machine yourself, and if you are really enthusiastic, you can shampoo it yourself, with care! The trick is not to wet the carpet thoroughly, but instead to lightly dampen it. A diluted wool detergent works, and a soft brush to brush the carpet gently, before blotting with kitchen paper and air drying it as quickly as possible. But if in any doubt, ask an expert.

The one thing that fills any carpet owner with panic is staining. The main thing is to deal with the stain quickly to minimise the damage. After that, the following instructions might help:

- Blot up as much of the stain as you can with kitchen paper – don't use anything else. Pour salt onto the stain, as it will absorb the wine (or whatever else may have caused the stain) – bicarbonate of soda does the same thing. But you have to do this immediately.

- For grease, bicarbonate of soda is the thing – sprinkled over the stain and left to absorb for a few hours, then vacuumed up.

- For pet 'accidents', either mix 50ml vinegar in 2 litres of water and spray onto the offending area, or do the same with laundry detergent, which is also good at removing stains and neutralising the smell. But for really persistent stains, you might need to use a specialist stain-removal product.

- Vinegar and a gentle detergent will help to lift coffee stains from carpets, but always blot the excess first.

- If you are unlucky enough to have a blood stain on the carpet – don't use warm water. Always use cold. Mix in a little washing-up liquid and spray it on the stain, before blotting again. You might have to do this a few times before the stain fades, so keep at it!

- Wood floors need care too, and as they come in all kinds of finishes, it's best to pick a specialist cleaner for hardwood floors. Some people will tell you that you can mop a hardwood floor, but I'd advise against it. If you do insist, make sure not to leave any standing water, as this will damage the floor. Another thing to avoid is scraping the floor with your vacuum cleaner attachment, so make sure that you have the soft brush down when you hoover.

WOOD AND LINOLEUM

Wood floors used to be solid – lovely – but not always easy to install and needing careful maintenance. A friend of mine, who is a DIY fan, installed his own solid-wood floor on a concrete base. It looked lovely, so off he went on holidays, happy as Larry, but he came home two weeks later to find a hill of wood in the middle of the living room. He hadn't left enough room for the wood to expand, so it had lifted. The moral of the story is, wood needs a bit of extra care when you are installing it – or, better still, get a professional to install it for you.

Nowadays, engineered wood flooring will offer you the look of wood, but with an 'engineered' base underneath it. You can get the top layer in a range of thicknesses, depending on your budget, and the advantage of this type of wood is that it's less pricey, less inclined to move, unlike solid wood, and is easier to install. However, like solid wood, it will show up marks and scratches, so you need to give it pretty much the same attention as solid wood, cleaning it carefully and oiling it regularly. Wood is high maintenance. In fact, now that I think of it, I can still remember my mother using a floor polisher – anyone remember those? They looked like a modern-day sander, except with three brushes at the bottom, which would rotate. Mum used to polish the hall three times a year, hanging onto the handle for dear life, and the smell of polish and the look of the shiny floor would be lovely. Of course, laminate flooring is much cheaper and easier to clean, but you won't get that 'real wood' look. However, nor will you get the 'real wood' cleaning and maintenance! Laminate has come a long way in recent years. Ideal if you want a quick change at a low price.

GREEN SHOOTS

The final touch to any room, as far as I'm concerned, is greenery. Many of us forget, when we're designing interiors, that plants can make such a big difference. I'm a plant person. I find that they really add something to a home – a sense of calm, a feeling that the home is truly lived in. Having said that, while I have a lovely garden in my home in Kerry, I am not at home enough to really look after house plants. Even the easiest house plant needs a bit of care, so if you don't have much time or are not a natural gardener, opt for the easiest of easy-care plants.

Did you know that the other great thing about house plants is that they can act as natural home purifiers? None other than NASA has researched which plants clean the air best. They did a study in the 1980s to see which plants might work best in space, but I'm sure they'd work equally well on earth!

- Aloe plants are very sturdy and they look good, and they also help to clean the air of chemicals emitted by certain paints and household cleaners. Tip: they do need lots of sunlight.

- Spider plants – remember them? These green-and-yellow-striped houseplants thrive in cool conditions – ideal for Ireland then! – and are hard to kill. They also do a great job of cleaning the air of things like carbon monoxide.

- Senseveria, or as we know it, Mother-in-Law's Tongue, is known for its long pointy green leaves, fringed with yellow – and, because they suck in carbon monoxide during the day and let oxygen out at night (the reverse of other plants), they are great to have in bedrooms. They will also manage well in gloom and without too much water.

- Golden Pothos or Devil's Ivy – great for hanging baskets, this greenish-yellow foliage is happy even in dim light – but be careful around pets and children – it's toxic!

- Ficus – this pretty tree is lovely in a living room, but it's not the easiest of plants to maintain. I had one once, and the leaves all fell off! However, if you are prepared to be careful and not to expose it to extremes of hot and cold it might be just the plant for you.

- Chinese Evergreen – is a really easy houseplant, with dark-and-light green oval leaves. It thrives in dim light, so will work just about anywhere in the house. The only thing it doesn't like is dry air, so mist the leaves with a water spray every now and again to avoid brown tips on the leaves.

- The Peace Lily – another easy-care plant with a really pretty white flower. It topped NASA's list for removing airborne pollutants in a room – and it's lovely to look at.

If you struggle to keep plants alive, here are a few that, according to *Good Housekeeping*, 'you can't kill'. Good news for those of us without green fingers. According to GH, the main culprits in plant destruction are over-watering and too much direct sunlight. Their advice is to sit your pots on a tray of gravel, so that they're not soaked in watery saucers. As a gardener myself, I've often found that plants like soil to be well drained, so I second this advice.

- Many horticulturists consider English ivy to be a pest, as it can get out of control, but if you confine yours to indoor hanging baskets, you'll be fine. It trails well and is hardy.

- The Dragon Tree is a pretty plant, with its red-tinged leaves. It will also thrive on the most basic of watering regimes – but don't get one if you have children or pets, as the leaves are toxic to both.

- The leaves of Calathea are almost zebra striped, with lovely stripes of green and maroon. They also don't mind poor light and need to be kept moist – but don't drown them! You might also know the variety called the Prayer Plant, because the leaves close together at night.

- You might remember rubber plants as the mainstay of the 1970s home. Their broad green leaves are lovely and they grow well in most conditions. They do attract dust, but all you need is to give the leaves a wipe with a damp cloth every now and again to keep them shiny.

- If orchids sound too scary for you, you'd be surprised at how easy they are to care for. All you need is to water them every week or so – and just a little water – keep them in a fairly moist environment and you are an orchid grower! I was given a present of an orchid years ago and I keep it on a windowsill out of full sunlight, where it seems to thrive.

- The aechmea, or Silver Vase plant is a lovely plant with silvery green leaves and a striking pink flower. It's easy to keep at home as it doesn't need much light, but you have to be careful about watering it: it has a little reservoir in the middle that quickly gets soggy and mildewed, so you'll need to empty this every so often to keep your plant healthy.

THE KITCHEN GARDEN

I think herbs are my favourite indoor plant, because they are easy to grow and when you need them, all you do is give a little snip and you have fresh herbs for dinner. What could be nicer? All you really need is a windowsill, and they'll save you money, as the plastic packs of fresh herbs in the supermarket can be expensive.

The hardiest herb plants are probably rosemary, sage and thyme, but these are best outdoors. I have a huge sage bush in my flower bed that is so hardy I have to prune it back vigorously every year. Sage has quite a distinctive taste, so not everyone loves it, but I find it great in stuffing and in rich, herby pasta sauces. The Italians love sage, and so do I!

I also have a very hardy thyme plant that I actually dug up once because it wasn't thriving; I stuck it in a gloomy corner beside the house, reminding myself to find a good spot for it later. It was a corner that got morning sun, but that was it, but after a couple of weeks, I noticed that my thyme plant was now thriving, and so I planted it in and left well alone – herbs always surprise me. The only spot that I've found hopeless is anywhere windy, so keep your herbs in shelter, by planting them against the wall of your house or in a sheltered part of your balcony. And don't take my example of the neglected thyme – most herbs like sun, which is why they thrive on windowsills and sunny balconies. As a rule of thumb, plants with smaller leaves, like rosemary and thyme, need more sun than those with big green leaves, like parsley.

If you are feeling brave, you can plant your herbs directly from seed in April or May, when there's no frost, but if you want a slightly easier life, you can buy them from the garden centre and plant them out. You'll need compost and also a pot that drains well. Be particular about your pots, because your herbs like well-drained soil. Terracotta is good, because it's porous, but keep an eye on herbs in terracotta, because they can dry out quickly. If you mix in some gravel with your compost, this will create nice drainage for your herbs.

When you pick your herbs, don't do so from the stem – just pinch or snip off a few leaves before a leaf intersection and your plant will continue to thrive. Feed them regularly with a good fertiliser and pick them regularly during the growing season. When you water them, do so at the base of the plant, but don't overwater or your plant might not grow well. As a rule, let the soil dry out a little before the next watering. If in doubt, stick your finger down under the surface of the soil to test for dampness. If it's dry, it's time to water.

You can grow herbs together in pots as well, if you like, but be careful about selecting them. Mint will go mad and take over whatever pot you plant it in, so beware. Some varieties, such as chives, mint and coriander like lots of water, so plant these together – don't plant them with herbs that don't like so much water, like rosemary, thyme or bay.

Rosemary is very easy to grow, but I'd plant it by itself, as I've found that mine thrives best alone; sage is also easy, but if you don't want a great big woody tree like mine, prune it regularly; I have always found basil and coriander the most difficult plants to grow successfully. My coriander tends to bolt no matter how often I pinch it out.

Basil hates our gloomy climate, and this might explain why I've had no success with the pots I've brought home from the supermarket. A quick bit of research tells me that I am better growing plants from seed, to get them acclimatised to the chilly Irish weather. It is also easy to overwater basil, according to the experts, and not to give it enough light. Basil really does need a sunny windowsill to thrive, with a bit of ventilation for good measure. Oh, and insects love basil, so keep a close eye out for whitefly and wash the leaves until these little pests are gone. Good luck!

Preserving herbs is a great idea, so that you can use them year round, and there are a couple of ways to do this. You can either dry them, or freeze them – yes, freeze them! They might not look as nice as fresh – in fact, don't be surprised if they look pretty mushy – but they will still keep their flavour for adding to soups and stews.

Drying works well with sturdy herbs like thyme, rosemary, sage and oregano, but not with delicate herbs like chives or basil, sadly. You simply wrap a little bunch in twine and hang it somewhere cool and dry for about a week. When they are dry, you can remove the leaves and pop them in an airtight jar. They'll keep for a few months this way – so you'll never have to feel guilty about wasting expensive herbs again!

Some chefs don't like the idea of freezing herbs at all, but if you are faced with a glut of, say, basil, parsley or coriander, you could give it away to friends, or you could try freezing – providing you don't want to use it like fresh herbs and just want to pop it in a pasta sauce. I discovered that there are a few recommended methods, for which I plan to try to see which works best. Note that the softer herbs don't freeze as well as the hardier ones.

- Wash the herbs and dry thoroughly. Lie little sprigs of herbs on a baking sheet and pop into the freezer until they are frozen, then either pop them whole into an airtight container, or chop finely and put into freezer bags. You can't really use frozen herbs much more than a couple of months past their freezing date. They won't look pretty, I'm told, but the herby flavour will still be worth it.

- You can also chop herbs and put into ice cube trays. I have found that you can either put them into the cube to about a quarter of the way up and fill with water – or fill with boiling water to blanch them and retain their green colour. You freeze these little ice cube trays in the freezer and, when you need them, simply pop a whole cube into your sauce. Handy!

- Another method involves placing your herbs in ice cube trays, up to about half full, and pouring either extra virgin olive oil or unsalted butter over them – you then have a herb butter/oil of sorts which you can add to sauces.

Of course, there are lots of uses of fresh and dried herbs at home, apart from cooking. I came across a lovely idea for home-made herb sachets that act as an alternative to mothballs, which I thought was a great idea. You'll need a mix of robust scented herbs, like rosemary and lavender, and you'll add cinnamon sticks, cloves and some cedar shavings to the mix, before putting them into those tiny little sachets that you can buy in craft shops and stationers. They are made out of organza and they aren't hard to find either in stores or online, where you'll find them described as 'favour bags', for those sugared almonds you get at weddings. They work equally well as mothballs though!

There's nothing nicer than dried lavender in bath soaks, in drawer sachets and even in food. Lavender ice cream is delicious! Also good is lavender tea, made by infusing lavender flowers and leaves with boiling water, which helps as a natural calming agent. If lavender tea sounds a bit 'out there' to you, you could mix it with something like chamomile.

One of my favourite ways of using mint is in natural mint tea. It couldn't be simpler: you just pour boiling water over a good few sprigs of mint and leave to steep before drinking. It's light and refreshing and great for indigestion. Parsley is also good – it's an excellent source of vitamin C, but also great for getting rid of garlic breath – chew a sprig and see!

Chamomile is excellent for digestion but also to soothe, which is why some people swear by a cup before bed. The dried flowers of the plant are infused with boiling water.

Garlic is an allium, like onions, but you'll see lots of wild garlic, which I'd describe as a herb. It's not hard to identify, with its pretty white flowers and glossy, narrow, green leaves. Garlic has endless properties, from digestion to heart health to fighting infection. Use garlic liberally in cooking – but perhaps not in tea!

When I go out for a walk, I occasionally come across someone picking nettles. I've never tried them, but when cooked, they taste like spinach, I'm told, and are a great source of iron. You could try nettle soup – the moment they are cooked they don't sting, by the way.

HOW TO ... DO HYGGE

You might have heard a lot about the Danish concept of 'hygge' recently. It's a term we don't have in the English language, but the closest thing to it would be 'cosy' – a way of looking at life that places value on little things that make life happy. Not money or stuff that we can buy, but rituals and ways of being that are comfy and relaxed and that we share with others. We could all do with a bit of hygge in our lives!

I like to drink my tea in a particular china cup when I'm at home, because it gives me a real sense of safety and peace – I'm at home in my own kitchen, looking out at the garden. I like to sit beside my Aga and be cosy and warm. That's hygge – and it doesn't cost me a penny.

Irish people could quite easily do hygge I think, because we are friendly and open, and we like our creature comforts: woollen blankets, fluffy slippers, warm mugs of tea – all very hygge. We also like to be around people, to share our time with others – not to mention our weather, which encourages us to sit indoors in front of a roaring fire. Yet, when the weather allows, we have a beautiful landscape to explore – also very hygge. In fact, Ireland is a hygge country, now that I come to think of it.

How can you bring the concept into your lives?

Get candles and a soft blanket in lovely Irish muted colours to throw over your knees.

Find a lovely **squishy cushion** or pillow case that just fits your head to rest on while you are reading your book.

Gather friends or family around the table for an easy supper – no posh dinner party needed – just soup, crusty bread, a big bowl of stew – good Irish food!

Banish the laptop and smartphone for the afternoon. I know, it sounds impossible, but you won't get that hygge feeling if you're stuck in front of a computer with a bright light shining in your face.

Sit in front of a warm fire, if you can. If you're in a bedsit or an apartment, you might not have an open fire, but all you really need is a warm blanket, a hot drink and a book in which to lose yourself.

Wrap up warm and take a walk outside in a park or in the country; just be in nature for a while. You have to do things properly though – no Irish wearing of a T-shirt in December! You need lots of warm layers to get that hygge feeling.

Enjoy the little pleasures in life – a warm bath, a cosy pair of socks, a nice woolly jumper, a hug from a friend – these are simple, don't have to cost anything and will make us feel better.

Live in the moment. Hygge is all about slowing down, resting and taking stock – what could be nicer in our busy, stressed-out world?

Surround yourself with things and people you love. You don't have to have lots and lots of stuff, just a few things that matter, and the people who matter in your life close by.

CHAPTER FOUR

The Littlest
Room in the
House

<><><><><><><><><><><><><><><><><><><><><><><>

'What is elegance? Soap and water!'

CECIL BEATON

A long time ago, when I was manager of the Victoria Hotel in Cork, we had a guest from Korea, who was on a trade mission with the IDA. One evening, he came down to reception and requested a wake-up call for the following morning. No problem, I thought, making a note of it for the night manager. About half an hour later, the chef ran into reception and told me that there was water pouring through the ceiling into the kitchen. I ran upstairs to the first floor to see where the damage might be coming from, and opened the door of the room over the kitchen to see water flowing down from the ceiling and big chunks of wallpaper hanging off the wall! I guessed that the leak had to be coming from the floor above, so I bounded up the stairs and knocked on the door.

Our Korean friend answered the door in a towel, looking mystified. 'Turn off the taps!' I yelled at him, before running downstairs to the kitchen to assess the damage. When I got downstairs, of course, the water was still pouring like a waterfall! So I bounded back up two flights of stairs and knocked on the door again. Now, this was in the days before keycards, so when he didn't answer, I let myself in. To my horror, the floor was covered in about two inches of water, but there was no sign of the guest. Gingerly, I made my way over to the twin beds and peered between them, in case he'd fallen there in a dead faint, but there was no sign of him. I feared the worst, that somehow he'd drowned in the bath, so I sloshed my way over to the bathroom door, and knocked loudly. 'Hello?'

I peered in the door and all I could see were the tops of two knees sticking out of the bath, which was overflowing nicely, water pouring onto the floor. 'Turn off the taps!' I shouted again, whereupon the two knees disappeared and the man leaned over and finally turned them off. By this stage, the room was awash and I was apoplectic. 'You eejit,' I shouted, unable to help myself, because half the hotel was saturated at this stage. The poor man was very apologetic and explained to me in lovely English that he'd assumed that there was an overflow and a drain in the bathroom, so that he could observe the same practice as he did at home – never to bathe in still water. As I learned from our chat, it's the norm to bathe in flowing water in Korea, and bathrooms there are fitted with a suitable drain and overflow system. He thought we did the same thing here! Is it any wonder I have a bit of a 'thing' about bathrooms?

I have devoted a chapter to this all-important room, because I think it's worth it. It's not just about hanging your toilet rolls in the correct way – although there is that! It's also about having a nice clean space to have your morning shower, to set yourself up for the day, or to be able to truly enjoy a relaxing bath at night, without staring at mould stains or grotty bathroom furniture. It doesn't have to be 'designer', as a few touches can add extra warmth to any bathroom. If you can't afford the best bathroom suites, perhaps you can splash out on some lovely bath oil or a nice big fluffy bath towel or scented candles to make things special. But all you really need to feel so much better and more relaxed is to have a clean and tidy bathroom.

Now, this chapter will be all about mould and smells, so I'll cheer you all up first by telling you a story about our handyman and the immersion. Mum had asked him to come to fit an immersion for her in the hot press or linen cupboard. We were only thrilled at the idea of being able to set it to heat water for showers – imagine the luxury. Anyway, he worked away and when he'd finished, off he went. The immersion worked beautifully and we were all delighted with it, but we couldn't understand why the phone kept ringing at random times of the day, and when we'd pick it up, there would be no one at the other end. This went on for months, until some bright spark found that the handyman had somehow managed to wire the immersion to the telephone, so every time someone turned the immersion on, the phone would ring!

I'll start with the basics, and something that is a common complaint in Irish bathrooms – mould. I know, perhaps this might put a bit of dampener on this chapter – excuse the pun! – but I firmly believe that if you get some of the foundations right for your special room, you will enjoy it so much more. Mould is the enemy of our lovely bathrooms, so we need to tackle it. It's unsightly, but, more importantly, it can be unhealthy. Many people react to mould, so it's best to minimise this household nuisance.

- Firstly, if you are doing up your bathroom, you can paint it with anti-mould paint – it won't keep this beastly thing away for ever, but it will keep it at bay and reduce it.

- Keep your bathroom as dry as possible. This might sound counter-intuitive, when you have clouds of steam rising from your shower or bath, but simply opening the windows after you shower or installing a good extractor fan will help to pull the moisture away quickly. So will wiping down damp surfaces after you use them.

- Regular cleaning can help to keep mould at bay. This might sound obvious, but I mean more than a quick rinse with water. After you bathe or shower, wipe the bath down with a squirt of vinegar and dry it, to prevent mould growth. Spray shower curtains, if you have them, with a vinegar solution to prevent mould, and every couple of weeks pop your shower curtains into the washing machine with, say, the bath mat. Regular spraying with diluted vinegar can really help with keeping mould down, so keep a bottle handy. But be aware that vinegar does not go with grout, so just be careful to spray it only on the bath or shower curtain.

- If grubby grout is your enemy, our old friend baking soda can help. Apply a mix of baking soda and washing-up liquid in a hot water solution to your bathroom tiles. And scrub! It's the scrubbing that really does the work, I think. A toothbrush or a special grout brush will be all that you need, plus some elbow grease! Only use diluted bleach (one part bleach to 10 parts water) in extremis, as it can damage tile grout. Cleaning grout could also give you another excuse to try your steam cleaner though! It's perfectly safe (as long as you don't scald yourself) and no chemicals are involved.

- For tiles, many of the mould-removing tips above will help, but some of us don't have standard bathroom tiles. We have mosaic – gorgeous, but tough to clean – or we might even have plastic! Be sure to use a cleaner that is designed for these tiles, because otherwise they might be damaged.

- A solution of baking soda, with a few drops of bleach added, applied as a paste to your grout and left for a little while – no longer than about 15 minutes – can then be scrubbed off with a toothbrush. If it refuses to budge after repeated applications, you may need to re-grout. If you are very handy, you might be able to do this yourself, but if not, you should call in an expert. Grout is one of those things that is hard to do, unless you are really very handy. Try elbow grease first, though!

- If your mould is growing on the ceiling or woodwork, diluted borax substitute or vinegar is more effective than bleach, as they attack deep-rooted mould. You'll need to use 250ml of borax substitute to four litres of water and to give the walls or woodwork a good scrub. And here's a tip: you don't need to rinse the borax off as leaving it on will help to prevent mould reccurring.

THE TUB

Now that we've got the nasties out of the way – at least, one of them! – let's have a look at bathroom 'furniture' itself and what is safe to clean on the different surfaces. It used to be that baths were all enamelled cast iron, as I well recall. Saturday night was bath night in our house and we'd race to get the bath over and done with, so we could sit in front of the TV and watch *The Monkees*! And we all shared the one fill of bath water – not nice if you were last to use the bath!

Of course now plastic or acrylic baths are commonplace, and you can even buy wooden or stone ones! There's nothing wrong with any of those choices, but they will require different cleaning products.

Acrylic baths are a popular choice nowadays, because they are light and comparatively cheap, but you can't let loose on your bath with abrasive cleaners. You'll need to use something gentle, like washing-up liquid applied with a soft brush. If you use it regularly, you can prevent gunge build-ups. If you have particularly resistant stains, ring your building or plumbing supplies store and ask them if they can recommend a specialist cleaner.

Enamelled cast-iron baths are the old-fashioned baths that we remember, and the modern free-standing 'clawfoot' baths are an example. They weigh an absolute ton, but they are hardy and easy to clean, as are their modern counterparts, *enamelled steel* baths: try the old favourite, bicarbonate of soda, mixed to a paste with a bit of water to wipe over your bath – no scrubbing, in case of damage – before rinsing away. Vinegar mixed with water – one to one – is also handy. Always check on a tiny area first, just in case.

If your bath stains are more resistant, try filling the bath with hot water, and mix in a handful of either biological washing powder or washing-up liquid. Leave to soak overnight and rinse off the next morning. You can use the same cleaning products on your sink.

For taps, shower handles, toilet handles and other chrome items, you want them to look shiny, but they can quickly get grubby, and sometimes even rusty. If you want to do some general cleaning of your chrome appliances, a little spray with Windolene and a buff with a soft cloth is just the job. Baby wipes also work for day-to-day maintenance, as does our old favourite, vinegar – a few drops squirted on a cloth or in a handy spray bottle will keep your taps and loo handle shiny.

A mix of baking soda and water, applied in a paste then rinsed off, is great for getting rid of soap scum on taps – where would we be without baking soda! If rust is an issue, as it often is with chrome, you might need to get the 'big guns' out! A mixture of equal parts salt and lemon juice can help to remove rust stains, as can a rub with steel wool. My favourite tip is for cleaning chrome appliances, particularly shower heads. Some experts tell you to unscrew the shower head and remove it, but this tip simply suggests that you wrap your shower head in a plastic bag, which you have filled with vinegar, and leave it for a few hours, before removing and rinsing to get rid of that fish-and-chip shop smell! Alternatively, you can unscrew the shower head, scrub it with an old toothbrush soaked in vinegar and poke into the little holes with a toothpick, before giving it a good soak in a vinegar bath.

If you have a shower in the bath, use a trap to keep hair from clogging the plug hole. If your bath is slippy, get a non-slip mat for it, but remember to lift it often to rinse soap scum away. Also important is to keep your glass shower door clean. You can do this by keeping one of those window-cleaning squeegees handy in the cabinet under the sink. A few wipes after every shower will keep your door clean. If you have ugly water stains, try rubbing the door with some bathroom cleanser, or even diluted washing-up liquid, and rinsing thoroughly before rubbing with a dry cloth to absorb all of the moisture. One thing we often have to do at the hotel is clean the shower-door hinges. All of that damp air creates moss, believe it or not.

CATHY'S TIP:

Make sure that your soap dishes have little perforations in them to prevent the build-up of horrible soap 'goo'.

BATHROOM SURFACES

Bathrooms can have all kinds of surfaces in them, from stone, to tile, to wood panelling, to just painted walls. Each surface needs a different kind of cleaning.

Those of you who have *stone* in your bathroom will know that it needs careful handling. It'll have been sealed but will need to be resealed once a year or so. The resealing is something you can do yourself, applying the solution and leaving it to dry. It may also have been treated with a specialist mildew repellent, which is good, because it is harder to clean stone – you can't use any of the harsh cleansers that work for other surfaces. The other thing that helps with mould and mildew is keeping your shower area as dry as possible, ventilating often and making sure the water drains away effectively. Stone is porous, so you have to avoid using acidic cleaners and also strong alkaline ones on the other end of the spectrum. A drop of washing-up liquid diluted in warm water is good for general maintenance, but as you'll have thought long and hard about natural stone for your bathroom, you will probably have bought a specialist cleaner to do the job.

Marble is something that people feel adds a little touch of luxury to bathrooms, but it's not that hard-wearing, so it's not for the faint-hearted! It also stains easily, so don't leave your nail-polish remover on the counter, or any perfumes or make-up. The same rules apply to it as to natural stone – no harsh cleaners: just a drop of washing-up liquid in warm water, wiped over the surface with a cloth. You won't be able to use any of your lovely home-made cleaners on marble, I'm afraid!

A practical, modern solution for bathrooms these days is *Corian®*. It's a synthetic surface that is hard-wearing and comes in a lot of colours. You'll be pleased to hear that you can use baking soda on it, but you really only need it for stains, as a wipe with a bit of washing-up liquid diluted in water will do the trick. It does show scratches, though. If you do have a scratch, rub it gently with fine sandpaper until it's smooth, then it's out with the car wax for a lovely shine!

IT HAS TO BE DONE

Now that your bath, surfaces and chrome are all gleaming, you can turn your attention to the least pleasant job – cleaning the loo. Most of us will use a squirt of toilet cleaner and a brush, God help us – but please don't! Brushes harbour nasty germs. If you must, I came across a handy tip: when you've finished brushing, flush the loo, then squirt a good amount of loo cleaner into the – clean – bowl. Stand your brush up in that and give it a good soak for half an hour.

But before we get ahead of ourselves, regular cleaning of the toilet bowl will prevent you having to attack it every so often. I like those little blocks that hang over the toilet rim. They smell okay – better than the alternative! – and they keep germs at bay, as does a daily squirt of a specialist loo cleaner. But if you want to give your loo a really good clean, fizz is your friend. Sprinkle a good amount of bread soda into the bowl, then squirt in your vinegar – and stand back! It *will* fizz. But that fizz is just what you need to give your bowl a good clean.

Vinegar is useful for spraying around the loo to get rid of stains – spray and scrub with a small brush (that you will dispose of afterwards!). There is also a bit of a myth that cola will clean the inside of your loo. No, I'm not joking. It's the citric acid, apparently. We haven't tried it in the hotel, needless to say ...

CATHY'S TIP:

Another loo-cleaning tip is to drop two denture tablets down the loo – leave them to fizz away before flushing.

Another unpleasant, but necessary task in the bathroom is unblocking the drain. I feel that something of the romance is taken out of this chapter with even the mention of drains! However, as many of you will know, it is a nuisance. Having one of those little traps in the plughole can really help, but every so often, there really is nothing for it but to attack the blockage with a specialist unblocker. However, if the thought of these nasty chemicals washing out into your water system is too much for you, you can make your own, with – yes, baking soda! It truly is the most handy thing. Mix 75g of baking soda with twice as much vinegar, and pour down the plughole. Leave for a few minutes and then rinse. Another handy drain unblocker – in fact, a handy product for any number of household tasks, is *soda crystals*. Sodium carbonate, to give it its scientific name, has all kinds of uses, from whitening grey whites, to cleaning the u-bend under the sink, to maintaining washing machines and dishwashers. You can find it in hardware stores.

BATHROOM BLISS

I heard on the radio recently that cleaning the bathroom ranks top of people's 'most hated' household jobs. It's hardly surprising, given what I've told you, but believe me, if you keep your bathroom clean, you can really enjoy it, instead of being afraid to go in to brush your teeth! And, more importantly, you can then turn your attention to the pleasures of having a nice clean bathroom, and the little extras you can enjoy. We might not all have marble bathrooms, but we can treat ourselves to a few luxuries to make life that bit nicer.

Let's start with loo paper. It's essential, of course, but who amongst us doesn't long for a bit of quilted comfort? I for one can still remember the horrible brown paper at school, and there is no room for that in my bathroom! Many of us like to buy recycled loo paper and that's great for the environment, but either way, buy the best that you can afford. There's nothing worse than scratchy paper to offend guests! If you want to know which brands are the most environmentally friendly, there are many websites, like www.theethicalconsumer.org, which will tell you everything you need to know.

There's nothing I like better than a lovely fluffy towel, and the same rule applies to towels as to toilet paper – buy the best that you can afford. We can't all have the poshest bath towels, but no matter what our budget, we can buy something durable and comfy. We have to buy a lot of towels for the hotel, as you can imagine, so I have become a bit of an expert.

Here's my handy guide to buying bathroom towels:

Towels come in lots of varieties, but the words you need to pay attention to are:

- GSM – this means 'grams per square metre'. The more GSM, the heavier the towel, because more cotton has been used to make it. You will see GSM ranging from 450 to the top end, 700–800. This will make it more absorbent, but also will take longer to dry.

- Zero twist – this means that the cotton in the towel has been woven without a twist in the yarn, so it's lovely and fluffy and it dries quickly.

- Egyptian/Suvin cotton – Egyptian cotton is self-explanatory; Suvin cotton comes from India and is extra soft.

- You might see other terms, like 'Cotton mix' – this means that another yarn has been woven into the towel. Cotton could be mixed with, say, polyester in less expensive towels, or you might even find bamboo woven into the cotton for extra strength. Cotton mix towels aren't necessarily the cheapest, although towels at the lower range do use less cotton. However, Egyptian cotton in particular has become more affordable, so you'd be surprised! I came across a number of budget ranges during my research that were offering the latest towel technology at very good prices, so shop around, and don't assume that the most expensive is the best.

- The weave also affects absorbency – a waffle pattern can make a towel more absorbent, and a jacquard weave or zig-zag pattern also looks lovely.

- Size does matter when it comes to bath towels. The standard size for a bath towel is 70 x 135cm, although this varies. Check before you buy that the bath towel is big enough – some are skimpier and you want to be able to wrap it comfortably around you. A bath sheet is bigger: 100 x 150cm. Some people find that this drowns them, so again, don't be afraid to check in the shop.

- No matter what kind of towel you buy, you can help it to last longer and be fluffier if you look after it. Every so often, wash your towels in a really hot wash to keep germs at bay – but just occasionally, so that you don't end up with cardboard towels! Don't use fabric conditioner with your towels as it makes them less absorbent – instead, put a clean tennis ball into the dryer with your towels if you are drying them that way – it really does work. If you prefer, you can also buy dryer balls – hard plastic knobbly balls that are specially made for the dryer. The best of all, though, is to line-dry towels for maximum freshness. That old favourite, vinegar, added to the rinse cycle in your washing machine will make your towels lovely and fluffy.

- Give everyone in the house his/her own bath towel, for hygiene reasons. No one wants your athlete's foot or any other nasties!

- Plain towels, without any embellishments on the fabric, will dry you more efficiently.

SOAP AND SALTS

Do you remember your granny used to collect all of the old bits of soap and glue them together into a horrible ball? You'd fight with your siblings not to be the one to have to use it! Soap was very basic, smelled medicinal and didn't foam particularly well. It was often associated with joyless washing.

Now, thankfully, soap has come a long way, and because animal fats are no longer used, thank God, we can enjoy a lot of plant oils, rather than harmful chemicals that dry our skin. When you are buying soap, or shampoo or any of a host of toiletries, you'll be aware of the word 'paraben'. Parabens are added to many toiletries to stop nasty things growing in them, but they were linked in one piece of research to potential breast cancer, and this resulted in a bit of a panic about them and a rash of 'paraben-free' labels on shampoos and soaps. As I read during my research, the link isn't conclusive, and the facts are quite a bit more complicated. The American Cancer Society has stated that using products with paraben in them does not increase the likelihood of developing breast cancer, but if you prefer to err on the side of caution, you might select something that has no parabens in it.

If you look at the back of a bottle of shampoo, you'll find a list of ingredients that would make your hair stand on end – excuse the pun! 'Surfactants' which are basically detergents, to help cleaning, or foaming agents like cocamide or cocamidopropyl betaine. Big words, but all these do is make a nice white foam which makes you feel that your shampoo is working – in fact, it makes no difference to the effectiveness of your shampoo. Apparently, it is we, the consumers, who have demanded foaming shampoos. 'Dimethicone' might make your hair sit flat, rather than frizz, and 'panthenol' is a fatty acid that will nourish your hair. These scary-sounding ingredients won't harm your hair because they are used in small quantities, but if you'd prefer something 'natural', look for shampoos that have fewer ingredients. Remember, though, that all cosmetic products need some kind of preservative to prevent bacteria growing in them. Also, some natural ingredients can actually be harmful to your skin, for example essential oils. It may be lovely to put in a burner to scent your bath, but it will irritate skin. However, natural oils like sunflower, coconut and evening primrose are good for your skin. I'm not an expert on skincare, so my advice would be to do your research. Don't make assumptions based on hearsay – examine the evidence for yourself and then make your choice.

On a less controversial note, I'm so delighted to see all of the lovely Irish products that are available for bath time nowadays, using ingredients like seaweed and milk – good Irish ingredients! Irish companies are doing so well nowadays, with lovely hand-made soaps that smell gorgeous and are an affordable bit of luxury, as are bath oils. Scented candles can also be a lovely bath-time treat, but don't light lots and lots of them. Apart from the fire hazard, inhaling all of the smoke isn't that restful! And, just as in cosmetics, check the labels carefully. And clear up any candlewax drips!

If you are looking to save some extra pennies by making your own bath products, there are lots of recipes. Making soap requires a number of specialist ingredients to help hold it together, but making your own bath salts is easy-peasy: an oatmeal bath is lovely and very soothing. All you have to do is grind porridge oats into powder in your food processor and pour them into your bath. Or you can add an equal amount of Epsom salts to the oatmeal and perhaps a little drop of Lavender essential oil. If you don't want bits of porridge floating in your bath, many craft shops and stationers have those tiny pot-pourri bags, which are perfect for your home-made bath soak. Honey is also lovely: a couple of teaspoons held under running water will make your bath lovely, without making you sticky! And, whilst essential oils shouldn't be rubbed directly on skin, a few drops of jasmine, ylang-ylang, lavender or eucalyptus oil poured into the bath will work wonders. Equal amounts of coconut oil and sugar make for a nice body scrub too.

Natural remedies for hair include eggs – beaten and massaged into the hair, they are a great natural conditioner – but rinse your hair thoroughly. Adding lemon juice to your rinse is great to brighten blonde hair, as is adding dried chamomile flowers. Apple cider vinegar makes a great rinse for darker hair, and for those of us with white hair, our old friend baking soda is back. You mix two tablespoons with the same amount of water, stir thoroughly, then massage this into your hair, before rinsing out. Then, you put 100ml of apple cider vinegar into a bowl or spray bottle with the same amount of water and spritz or soak your hair in the mixture. Again, rinse out. This treatment is a natural alternative to white-hair shampoos and is great at keeping yellow tinges at bay.

I've included some natural recipies in my Almanac (see page 181) for further reading.

HOW TO ... MAKE YOUR OWN BATH SALTS

Home-made bath salts can be a mix of **rock or sea salt**, including most natural salts (not table salt) and **Epsom salts** (great for soaking tired muscles). Try two parts Epsom salts to one part salt (rock, sea or Himalayan), adding in half a part of baking soda.

You can add a few drops of an **essential oil** like lavender. Be careful with essential oils though. Never use them without checking if you are pregnant, ill or have broken skin. Some essential oils, like clove or bay, citronella or oregano, have been associated with skin reactions. The National Association for Holistic Aromatherapy (www.naha.org) has conducted research in the area of essential oils, and their findings are worth reading if you'd like to know more.

CHAPTER FIVE

The Linen Cupboard

*'Don't you just love those twelve seconds
when all the laundry is done?'*

UNKNOWN

At the hotel we have a huge linen cupboard, as you can imagine, because crisp linen is a must for all of the bedrooms. Our sheets have a thread count of 300 – which might not mean anything to you, but the higher the thread count, the softer and crisper the sheet. We have them laundered regularly – of course – and when they come back from the laundry, we have to leave them to cool down for a whole day. You might not know this, but linen retains heat, and if we were to put them in the linen cupboard right away, they'd go on fire!

Of course, growing up in Balally, we didn't have 300-thread-count sheets and huge linen cupboards, but Mum used to spend a lot of time doing the laundry. It really was a terrible chore in those days, with the twin tub and the mangle and the unpredictable Irish weather, and she always had to make sure that Dad got a clean shop coat every day – just like the ones they wore in Lipton's supermarket – either white or beige, which had to be washed and pressed and ready.

Recently, when I was thinking about that awful chore, I remembered the Victorian rhyme about laundry:

> *They that wash on Monday*
> *Have all the week to dry.*
> *They that wash on Tuesday*
> *Are not so much awry.*
> *They that wash on Wednesday*
> *Are not so much to blame.*
> *They that wash on Thursday*
> *Wash for every shame.*
> *They that wash on Friday*
> *Wash in sorry need.*
> *They that wash on Saturday*
> *Are lazy folks indeed.*

Some endings of this rhyme are less polite: 'Oh, they are sluts indeed'. It's easy to see how poorly some people were regarded if they didn't do their washing! Another interesting insight into the washing day came to me from the Herbert Hoover library archive: 'Washing the family's clothes was often done on Mondays, and it took the entire day. First water was heated in a metal boiler on a cookstove or in the fireplace. When the water came to a boil, soap shavings were added and the water was stirred until the soap dissolved. Next the clothes were dumped in. First the whites were washed, then the colored clothes, then the heavy work clothes. The clothes boiled for ten minutes and were then removed and rubbed with home-made soap and scrubbed on a ribbed washboard. After all the clothes had been washed the tub was filled with fresh water to rinse the clothes with.' Imagine the sheer drudgery of it all!

Thankfully, nowadays, with easy-care fabrics and washing machines with lots of settings, doing the laundry isn't quite as much of a task – but it can be a battle, particularly for those of us with families, when the washing machine is on the go all of the time and it hardly seems that something is ironed when it's back in the wash again! So, while we all know that there really is nothing nicer than crisp, clean laundry and fluffy towels, life sometimes gets in the way. This chapter will look at simple, easy ways to keep your laundry fresh, clean and smelling lovely.

BEFORE WASHING

Before you even get to putting a load in the washing machine, take a look to see if anything needs repairing, such as a button sewn back on a shirt or a hole mended. It's much easier to do this before you wash. Those of you who think you haven't a clue how to darn or sew on a button might be surprised at how easy it is. All you need are the basics. If you know these, you will be able to do most repairs yourself, saving yourself money – and you'll be quite proud of your new skills!

HOW TO ... SEW ON A BUTTON

While I was researching this book, I came across a website called The Art of Manliness (www.artofmanliness.com), which gives very good instructions on sewing on a button. It's time to learn, men!

Get yourself one of those handy little sewing kits that come in a plastic box. You can find these anywhere nowadays, in garage shops or convenience stores. They'll have a row of threads in a few colours, a nail scissors, a measuring tape, a couple of needles and pins and possibly one of those needle-threading gadgets to make the whole process a bit easier. It's a metal circle with a loop attached, with which you push the thread through the needle.

Pick a thread in the same colour as your outfit if at all possible, or at least one that doesn't stand out.

Thread the needle by holding it up in front of you. I turn my needle slightly side on, so that I can judge where the thread meets the hole and pull it through – making sure that I'm wearing my reading glasses. If you really struggle, use the threading gadget. You push your thread through the loop in the gadget and then insert the loop into the eye of the needle and pull through. Threading is the hardest bit, so once this is done, you are away in a hack.

Pull through a good 20cm of thread – long enough to be able to pull a few times through the button holes, but not so long that it gets tangled up in a big knot! If in doubt, pull your thread through and double it, so that the thread will be stronger. This is great for buttons – you won't need it for hems or patching. Tie a knot in the end of your single or double thread by simply making a loop – wrap the thread around your finger and push the end of the thread through, then tie. This will stop your thread simply pulling through the hole and coming out again.

Lift the dress/shirt/coat towards you and find the place where the button was originally sewn on. There will usually be a little bit of thread hanging or a mark in the fabric. If there isn't, it's time for you to make one! All you need to do is push the needle and thread through to the other side and then back – and then again – so you have a little mark to indicate where the button should go. You'll need just a tiny stitch here. If you are feeling particularly confident, or are in a desperate hurry, you can omit the stitch and just line the button up with the others on your garment.

With one hand, **place the button at the spot** and hold with your thumb on the button and your finger underneath the fabric.

Take the needle and thread in your free hand and push it from underneath the fabric through one of the holes in the button, holding the button in place with a finger. You'll only need to do this twice for the button to stay in place, so be patient! Once the thread is through one hole, pop a pin into the gap, before pushing the needle back through the opposite hole. This will stop you pulling the thread through so tightly that the fabric puckers. (You'll be taking the pin out at the end.) Push the needle back into the opposite hole, through the fabric to the underside, pulling the thread fully through, then begin the process again. This you will do until the button is securely sewn back on. Hey presto!

Once you have completed this process, **it's time to tie off your thread**. This you do by firstly removing the pin, then lifting the button slightly and wrapping your thread around the thread that you have sewn. Then you push the needle back through the fabric to the underside and, in the little knot you'll have created underneath, push the needle through it a few times, before snipping the thread off with the scissors. A four-hole button requires the same process, but with each pair of buttonholes, so repeated twice.

Give yourself a pat on the back!

HOW TO ... TIDY UP A HEM

I don't propose to turn this chapter into a dressmaking class, you'll be glad to know, but there may come a time when you pick up your favourite pair of jeans or trousers and notice that the hem has come loose. Time to get your sewing kit out again! This is really not difficult. The only thing you have to remember is to sew so that the stitching doesn't show on the outside. So ...

Turn your trousers inside out and locate the loose hem.

Place the leg of the trousers on a flat surface and find where the loose thread of the hem is. Many trousers now come with just a flat seam on the bottom with thread sewn into a zig-zag pattern. You won't be able to achieve this without a sewing machine, so for your quick repair, just pin the little gap where the thread has come loose about half-way between the bottom and the top of the hem. Then thread your needle – you'll be an expert now! – and begin. What you want to do with hemming is not push your needle all the way through, but simply 'pick up' a few threads. So you push your needle through the folded bit of the fabric, pulling from back to front – i.e. pushing the needle in and pulling it towards you. Then you pick up a few threads from the fabric above the hem, before moving along a little bit and pushing the needle through the fold again. Repeat until the gap has been covered, then tie off.

As you pick up your threads, turn the leg inside out for a moment to check that the thread isn't showing on the outside, then continue.

If this sounds too complicated, **try using a little bit of hemming tape**. Instead of sewing, you can simply pop in a section of this handy tape – which is readily available – under the hem of your garment and press it with an iron. Two things to be aware of here: if you press the tape for too long, you'll end up with a shiny iron mark on your trousers/jacket. But if you don't press it for long enough, the tape won't stick! I like to use a clean tea towel between the iron and the garment to avoid shine. The second thing about hemming tape is that it can wash away gradually, leaving you with the same problem as before, so perhaps only use it in a bind.

EASY PATCHING

There might come a time when you pick up your favourite jumper or pair of jeans and discover that you have a hole in the elbow or knee. Not to worry – you can repair it yourself.

For your jumper, you can darn the hole, as long as it's small. Turn your garment inside out and, using a thread of the same colour, 'pick up' the threads on one side of the hole then the other, until you have – very gently – pulled the two sides of the hole together. Don't pull the thread too tightly, or you'll end up with a puckered mark instead of a hole! Before you tie off the hole, turn your jumper the right way around to check that you've fully sewn the hole shut, then tie off. Turning your garment the right way around, smooth out any puckering. It won't be perfect, but a tiny ridge is better than a big hole.

Using hemming or webbing tape is also good if you want a quick fix, but it really only works with small holes. Turn your garment inside out, then place a square of hemming tape over the hole, making sure that you have pushed as many strands of thread across it as possible. Iron the hemming tape as you would normally – through a clean towel. When you turn your garment right side out, you'll see that your hole has been neatly patched.

THE WASHING MACHINE

Now that you have repaired any damaged clothing, you just want to stuff it all into the machine – right? If you are tempted, pause for a second and think about whether there are any of your clothes that you might not actually need to wash. It might seem tempting to just throw everything in, but you want your nice new top to last as long as possible, and your jeans to keep their shape, so don't be in such a hurry.

I discovered that in 2014, the CEO of Levi's, Chip Bergh, advised customers that jeans shouldn't really be washed – and that he hadn't washed his in a year! This might make your hair stand on end, not to mention your dirty jeans – but the point is that over-washing will just loosen the jean fibres and cause the dye to fade more quickly, so keep washing to a minimum. If your jeans get stained, just treat the stain itself, and air dry them so that they don't get smelly. Some people swear by putting jeans in the freezer overnight to kill bacteria – and you could try this: I did come across an experiment which concluded that freezing jeans didn't seem to result in more bacteria than not freezing them, which isn't exactly a ringing endorsement!

The best way to keep jeans fresh is to air dry them and just spot treat stains as they arise. If you must wash your jeans, look for a specialist 'dark wash' detergent to maintain the dye in your jeans.

Silk is another fabric that does not benefit from over-washing, or indeed any washing at all – but that really depends on colour fastness. The Silk Association of Great Britain recommends that you do a little patch test before deciding whether your silk garment is washable. You simply moisten a little section of it and place it on a white towel, then you press it gently with an iron. If colour leaks onto the towel – it's not colour fast, so get it dry cleaned.

If it is colour fast, only use a very mild washing powder/liquid – one that has been specifically designed for woollens and delicate fabrics. Wash gently before rinsing and rolling in a towel to soak up extra moisture. Then hang to dry. No vigorous scrubbing or rubbing, please, because this damages the fabric. And be careful when ironing it: no steam, which can give you water stains on your lovely silk.

CATHY'S TIP:

If you get water stains on delicate fabrics, immerse them in water for a few minutes, then dry and start again.

Woollens and cashmere also require delicate handling and use of specialist detergents. Use lukewarm water only and don't vigorously scrub the garments – a gentle swish is all you need. Rinse gently with cool water then squeeze – not by twisting it, which might damage it, but by pressing it very gently into a ball shape and then squeezing. You can roll your jumper in a towel to absorb excess moisture before drying. I saw a great tip about popping your sweater into a colander and letting the moisture drip out – genius! Dry your wool garments flat to prevent them losing shape.

STAIN REMOVAL

Many garments will last longer if you wash them less often. Of course, you want to be hygienic, but you may not need to use the washing machine quite as often as you'd think. You can simply refresh your clothes or apply quick stain removal, rather than going the whole hog and using the machine.

If you are in a terrible rush and discover that your nice sweater is looking a bit tired, but that you really, really need to wear it, try using laundry sheets – those fragranced sheets that you add to the washing machine – popping one into the dryer for a few moments with your garment and giving it enough of a spin to let the fragrance settle into the fabric. A little spritz with a fabric spray will have the same effect.

The other quick fix for laundry refreshing is to spray with a 1/1 mix of vinegar and water and then hang out to dry. I have heard of some people using the same approach with vodka, but care is needed with staining delicate fabrics – so stick with the laundry sheets! Of course, these are just emergency fixes, but they can be effective.

If you have food or other stains on your clothes, here are some quick ideas to clean them before you wash:

- Sweat stains on underarms can be removed by soaking in a mix of equal parts water and lemon juice, giving the stain as strong a rub as you can (this depends on the material) before hanging it out to dry: the sunlight will help with removing the stain. Then, put into the wash. If the stains are stubborn, *Good Housekeeping* recommends a solution of equal parts glycerine and water – leaving to soak for an hour before placing in the machine with your detergent and an enzyme-based cleaner.

- If your perspiration stains are smelly, a solution of borax substitute (two teaspoons to 500ml water) will help as a pre-soak before washing.

- Make-up stains can be treated with a squirt of shaving foam before popping into the washing machine.

- Lipstick stains can be treated with a squirt of hairspray before popping into the wash.

- Has your biro leaked in your shirt pocket? You could use a specialist stain remover, but try a solution of methylated spirits first. Check to see if the stain has soaked through to the actual shirt, and if not, slip your hand into the pocket before dabbing at the stain with a cotton wool ball soaked in methylated spirits – don't be too free and easy with it as you might make the stain spread. (And check that your fabric is colour-fast, as methylated spirits can affect this.) Soak up the ink as it leeches out of the fabric with white paper towels until no more ink comes out, then rinse in cold water. Do this a few times until you've got as much ink out as you can. If your shirt is colour-fast, you can use an oxy-action cleaner for any traces of ink that remain – but check the label first!

- There can be nothing worse than grass and mud stains, but they are a fact of life if you have sporty people in the house. First, soak the stains in cold water. I know, you might think hot is best, but for this type of stain, cold is the thing. Now, try using a few drops of your washing-up liquid or detergent as a stain remover. Soak it in and leave it for a while before washing. If it's a particularly stubborn stain, rubbing alcohol or hairspray can work. Rubbing alcohol is available from your chemist, not as freely as in the US, but it is effective with certain types of stain. Dab some onto the stain before using your pre-treater.

- Tea and coffee stains can be 'lifted' with club soda, before running under cool water, then dabbing on a touch of your normal detergent. Washing with biological powder is best for removing tea and coffee stains.

- For bloodstains, a good long soak in cold water is the thing, before covering the stain with detergent and rubbing it away. Then wash as normal. Don't let hot water near bloodstains as it will 'set' them.

- Ketchup stains are a fact of life if you have children. Try removing them by running under cold water, then soaking the stain in your washing detergent and leaving for a good half an hour. If the stain isn't gone, apply a good amount of white vinegar and leave for a bit longer, then rinse again and wash as normal.

Now that you have your lovely, mended, pre-treated clothes, all you have to do is put them into the washing machine, but you'll find that your machine works a lot more smoothly if you look after it.

Keep the door open a little bit between washes to let air circulate, but be careful here: Curious cats and small children should not be allowed anywhere near washing machines.

Keep the soap drawer clean by pulling it out and washing it every now and again. You shouldn't need to yank it out, just a gentle tug, before washing and replacing.

Every now and again, run a hot cycle in your washing machine without clothes, to clean the machine. A cup of bleach loaded into the machine before your hot cycle will help to keep mould and mildew at bay. Less abrasive but also good is a cupful of vinegar added to the detergent drawer. Mind your hands when you do this – wear rubber gloves!

SORTING LAUNDRY

I like the poem 'Sorting Laundry' by Elisavietta Ritchie, because it gives an idea of all of the things that can go through our minds when we are busy with practical activities. If you just hate sorting the laundry, hopefully these few lines will help you to see that it can also be good thinking time.

Folding clothes,
I think of folding you
into my life.

So, maybe sorting laundry isn't that boring after all! However, it is necessary, because if you sort your whites from your darks, your synthetics from your cottons and delicates, you'll keep your clothes in as good a condition as possible. If you have the room, invest in a laundry sorter. Unfortunately this won't actually sort your laundry for you – wouldn't that be great? – but simply has separate compartments in it for whites, colours and delicates. They are large, though, so you might find a basket a better option – you can get ones that fit in a corner, or even better, laundry bins that come with holes in the bottom for ventilation. I have also seen DIY laundry sorters, a row of plastic baskets that fit onto little runners in the corner of a bathroom or utility room. What a great idea. If your budget doesn't stretch to posh laundry bins with compartments, a small canvas laundry bin is lovely – and some are so cheap that you could even buy two, one for whites and one for coloureds.

I feel that children need to know how to do their own laundry at a reasonable age. I know that some people like to put a laundry basket in each bedroom, so that children learn to put their laundry into the basket, rather than on the floor, which is a great idea. But rather than collecting the baskets yourself and sorting, get your kids to do it! On designated days, they have to bring their laundry baskets into the utility room, or even to a spot in front of the washing machine, and divide their clothes into whites and coloureds.

Of course, you'll also want to divide your washing into types of fabric, so that, for example, your jeans can all go into a relatively cool wash with the appropriate washing liquid. Or all of those nylon-mix school jumpers can be washed at 30 degrees. This is all the kind of thing that you can teach children as you go along. With so many parents working nowadays, it makes sense to share the household chores, and the sooner you begin this process the better.

Things you'll need to teach them include:

- **Checking that they haven't left anything in their pockets – essential with children. I have a friend who washed her son's games console, because it had been left in his jeans pocket, so always get them to check!**

- **Looking at the care label to see what temperature the garment will need to be washed at.**

- **Removing items that need special care and putting them to one side.**

- **Sorting whites from coloureds.**

- **The basic wash cycle buttons on the washing machine, and what speed spin the clothing will need.**

- **Where to put in detergent and fabric conditioner.**

- **How to close the door properly.**

- **To know when a cycle is finished and when it's safe to open the door.**

They won't get the hang of this immediately, of course, and you don't want small children fiddling with the washing machine, but older ones would certainly benefit from laundry lessons. Over time, they will become more competent, and hopefully, by the time they are teenagers, they'll be able to sort and load their own laundry – wouldn't that be great?

CATHY'S TIP:

Familiarise your children with the dryer if you have one, but don't let them use it for drying one T-shirt or a pair of socks! Remind them always to clean out the lint drawer.

WASHING TIPS

Assuming that you know how to operate a washing machine, what special tips will keep your whites white and your colours coloured? How do you stop your favourite top from fading and getting baggy?

Keeping whites white is important and yet tricky at the best of times. Water quality is certainly a factor, not helped by the fact that many of us don't separate, say, towels from other white items, so everything ends up a kind of dingy grey! I find that being meticulous about separating the different kinds of whites really works. For example, if I washed my towels with my white T-shirts, I couldn't actually wash them at a high enough temperature, so keep all whites that can be washed in a hot wash together and so on.

For towels and sheets, grey is never a good look, and nor is it attractive in underwear, so how can you preserve their whiteness?

- **Try a dishwasher tablet. Add one to your detergent drawer before you wash, or soak your clothes in water with a diluted tablet for an hour or so before putting them into the wash. This makes whites white – but be aware that it's probably not suitable for those with sensitive skin.**

- **Adding a cup of white vinegar to the rinse cycle helps, because the acidity breaks down food stains and your whites will brighten too.**

- Soaking your clothes in lemon juice or adding half a cup of lemon juice to your wash cycle can also help, and is particularly good if you plan to line-dry your clothes – although there is more work involved in squeezing all of those lemons!

- Many people swear by 'oxy' products as brighteners and they are certainly good at removing stains, but be careful about using them on delicate fabrics. Many of these cleaners include bleach, which will most certainly brighten whites, but it might also leave spots on the fabric, as well as being not so great for the environment. Alternatives to bleach include vinegar, lemon juice and baking soda. Half a cup of baking soda added to your water might not be as effective as other cleansers in whitening, but it will soften and freshen your laundry and is gentle on the environment.

- For grey tea towels, try soaking them in a pot with lemons overnight, then giving them a good old boil wash. They'll be brighter and they'll smell nice!

- My mother used a laundry 'blue' agent to keep whites white. It was a kind of solid block which could be tied into a little laundry bag and put into the wash. It can still be found online, if you are keen (try www. oldandinteresting.com). Modern washing detergents use brighteners which have made laundry blue largely redundant – but it's worth a shot!

MATCHING PAIRS

Odd socks are the bane of many a person's life, but how on earth can we keep them together? I was very amused to read about the 'Sock Loss Index', compiled by two scientists recently to try to explain why socks go missing in the wash all of the time. Apparently, the average person loses 1.3 socks per month, so, 15 socks a year! It has to do with a lot of factors, including careless laundry sorting and the 'complexity' of the washing, combined with the fact that we are, apparently, a bit lazy about trying to locate missing socks, giving up pretty quickly if we can't find them.

I remember buying little plastic feet from one of those door-to-door salespeople many years ago. Each foot had two holes in it with plastic teeth, and the idea was that you'd pull a sock through each hole, so that they'd stay together in the wash. Not a bad idea, even if a bit too labour-intensive for me! A little mesh laundry bag, of the kind that delicate underwear is washed in, can also be useful for keeping socks together – but make sure that you have nothing in your bag that will run in the wash.

Plastic clips, the kind that you see on sandwich bags, are also good: simply clip your pairs of socks together before popping into the wash. Or, indeed, you can pop a rubber band around your pairs of socks – effective, and the band won't usually come off. Alternatively, make sure that you sort socks as soon as they come out of the wash, to avoid headaches – or insist on only buying socks of a particular colour. But lost socks are, I'm afraid, a fact of life!

More annoying and destructive are colours that run in the wash, destroying a whole load. To prevent colours running, wash at the coolest temperatures that you can get away with. If you suspect that you have a garment that might run, test a patch first with a damp white paper towel. If any dye comes away, don't put this garment in with a load – wash it separately.

However, if you've just removed your load of washing from the machine, and have found that it's all pink or blue, locate the culprit and remove it, then put your washing back in. Add a half cup of vinegar to the drawer – and pray! Alternatively, you can add an oxygen-based bleach to your detergent drawer – but this is harsh on delicate fabrics. A colour-run remover will also be effective, and can be purchased in bargain stores and supermarkets. The main thing to avoid is tumble drying the load, as the run will 'set' and it will be harder to remove.

DRYING

Line-drying is one of the best ways of brightening your clothes, and it's also a cheap, environmentally friendly way of drying your washing. But of course, Irish weather dictates that this isn't always possible – how many of us spend a morning looking anxiously out at the sky for any sign of rain, or spend our time dashing in and out of the house, clothes in hand?

On the other hand, using a tumble dryer can be expensive in terms of electricity and also harder on clothes. Whatever you decide, avoid the steaming radiators if you can possibly help it – or indeed drying your clothes indoors, as this can produce a lot of mould. Not good for our lungs! I came across a piece recently which found that mould poses a potential risk to youngsters, the old and asthma sufferers – but indoor dampness is probably not good for any of us. Try to find some indoor spot like a garage for drying to avoid this problem. Make sure that this spot is well ventilated to prevent mould spores building up.

There really is nothing nicer than a line-dried sheet or towel – they have a freshness that just can't be equalled by that slightly airless smell you get when you take them out of the dryer. Don't forget not to hang woollens on the line, though, because they will lose their shape. Dry them flat. I'm also told that duvets or sleeping bags shouldn't be hung from a clothesline, because the filling will sink to the edges. Fair enough, but you can't really tumble dry duvets (unless you like to burn money!), so, again, hang them as flat as you can – use a clothes horse, or, alternatively, turn them often.

When you are hanging your sheets out to dry, fold them over the line, hem side up, and pin the hems by the corners – this way, you avoid having peg marks in the middle of your sheets. Dresses should be hung by the shoulders, or you can put them on a hanger and hang that from the clothesline. Hang skirts by the hem. Hang shirts by the tail and open for best drying. Hang socks by the toe and fold undies over the line and pin. Try not to pull clothes out of shape and if you have a big heavy item, rig up some kind of double clothesline or rest some of it on a drying rack, so that it doesn't sag.

If you can't dry clothes because of the weather and you have a tumble dryer, you can save money on drying costs by putting a dry, fluffy bath towel in with the damp clothes. Don't overfill the dryer, because the load will take ages to dry and will cost more – and your clothes will have more wrinkles. Watch your heat settings on your tumble dryer. Fabrics like cotton can be dried on a hotter setting, but synthetics and knits will need a lower temperature. I like to try to line dry as much as possible, and just finish my towels and sheets in the dryer. Tumble drying does help with the board-like quality of line-dried towels!

Don't use fabric softener when you are washing towels, because this makes them less absorbent, but if you don't want cardboard towels, pop a couple of – clean – tennis balls into the dryer. They really do work to make towels soft and fluffy. And one final thing: always, always empty the lint drawer between dries. It really will make your drying more efficient as well as safer.

CATHY'S TIP:

Instead of spending money on expensive freshening sheets, make your own by cutting scraps of old fabric, like towels or T-shirts, into little squares. In a bowl, mix a cupful – 200ml or so – of vinegar with a few drops of lavender essential oil, then dip your fabric squares into the solution, before storing them in sealed jar. Place a squeezed-out square in the tumble dryer with your wash – and, hey presto, a lovely smell!

THE LINEN CUPBOARD

Once you've emptied your dryer and taken the clothes off the line, it's time to open the linen cupboard – to find that a whole lot of things crash out on top of you! How many of us store all kinds of things in our hot presses or airing cupboards? Ironing boards, vacuum cleaners, laundry baskets ... often other things creep in, too: the table cloth that's only used at Christmas, bathroom supplies, the mop and bucket. Before you know it, your linen cupboard can become home to a whole host of clutter. However, with just a few small adjustments, it can be a joy, with everything you need for bed and bathroom at your fingertips. Here are a few hints to help you to organise your linen cupboard:

- **Get someone handy to drill a hook onto the back of your linen cupboard door for you to hang the ironing board. Many DIY stores also have a handy wire storage rack for the iron, so you can keep it above the board.**

- **Buy plastic storage boxes to keep toilet rolls and bathroom accessories tidy. Keep your loo rolls handy, so that you don't have to rummage through everything to find them.**

- **Buy shelf dividers so that you get more from your shelves and can store an extra layer of things at mid-level.**

- **Store the things you use the least up high, where you only occasionally need to wander.**

- **Think about whether you really do want to keep Aunty Maeve's linen tablecloth on a shelf at the top of the hot press – you could store it somewhere more convenient, so that you have it to hand when you're having a dinner party.**

- **Roll towels into Swiss roll shapes, rather than storing them folded flat. This means that you can take a towel out of the pack without the others all tilting sideways!**

- Fold your matching sheets and duvet covers and pop them inside the relevant pillowcase, so that you can find the whole set when you need it. Look at keeping groups of items in handy bags: that set of sleeping bags that you use for camping holidays can be stored in a tied laundry bag, for example, or your holiday swimming togs can be kept in a tied sports bag.

- Buy vacuum bags for summer/winter duvets, as you can store quite a lot in the bag once the air has been sucked out of them. The same goes for blankets and comforters. Do this seasonally.

- Every so often, sort through sheets and towels in your linen cupboard and discard any sheets that are too worn to use any more. You can also store old towels or cloths that you might use for dusting.

- Think about how many sheet/duvet sets you really need. Three is about right, I think. One for the bed, one for the washing machine and another as spare. Any more will fill your linen cupboard with rarely used 'stuff'.

- Keep a separate shelf for: duvet/sheet/pillowcase sets; towels, cleaning equipment, medicines (a high shelf is advisable for these and they should be kept in a box that can't be opened by little hands).

Now that you have your linen cupboard just the way you want it, all you have to do is to learn how to fold your sheets and duvets to minimise creasing.

I can still remember folding sheets with my mother, long before the days of duvets. We had to stand across from each other, hands out wide, a corner of the sheet in each hand. Then we'd fold the corners to the middle, then grab the bottom of the sheet and fold that to the top. We'd have a long rectangle of sheet left, and we'd have to walk towards each other, me handing her my two corners to match hers. She would fold the now halved rectangle into a smaller one and – we were all set! The only problems that arose were with fitted sheets, which were awful things to fold.

Of course, we use lots of fitted sheets at the hotel, so I've had plenty of practice in folding these tricky items. I thought I had the knack, until I stumbled across a very handy Martha Stewart tutorial recently, which had an excellent method which I've been using ever since. Basically, you begin with your sheet inside out, a hand in each of the two top corners of the sheet. You fold the corner in your right hand onto the corner in your left. Then you run your hand down the elastic of the sheet until you find the next corner, which you then flip up onto the other two corners in your left hand, and then you do the same thing with the final corner. You will end with all four corners folded onto your left hand, right side out. You then lay the sheet flat, and flip the flat ends over onto the neatly folded corners. It's terrific!

I know that some of you will have seen my attempts to fit a duvet cover onto a duvet and had a good laugh about it, but believe it or not, I do know how to do this! The way I usually do it is to lay the duvet flat on the bed, turn the cover inside out, push my arms into the far corners of the cover, then reach down and take a corner of the duvet in each hand. I then lift the duvet – with the cover now attached to the top and flip it until the rest of the cover shakes down to the end. Next I go to the other end of the duvet and push the corners into the duvet cover, before zipping or buttoning it and giving it another little shake. However, in the course of my research, I've also discovered another way of doing this, which I'll have to try on live television! It's called the 'California Roll' and this is how it goes:

- Take your duvet cover and turn it inside out.

- Lay the cover on the bed flat, open end on the opposite side of the bed.

- Lay your duvet on top of the cover, matching the corners.

- From the closed end, roll your duvet cover/duvet all the way until you reach the open end. You should now have a duvet cover/duvet 'sausage'.

- Hold one side of the open top of the duvet against the duvet inside, then tuck the other side under the sausage.

- Turn the sausage over and button or zip the cover closed.

- Start to unroll the sausage again. You'll now find that you have a duvet-covered sausage that you unroll all the way up the bed to the top.

- Lie down and have a little nap after all of that!

IRONING

There's nothing I like better than a freshly ironed shirt. It's essential to the way I look, but it also feels great. Ironing shirts in particular always reminds me of Phil Coulter. Now, in case you think I've gone mad altogether, it's because I can still recall burning one of his shirts! He'd come to Killarney to do a few nights in the Gleneagle Hotel, and he'd decided to stay with us at the Park. On the day of his first concert, he sent down a number of shirts to be ironed. These were no ordinary shirts, but heavy stage shirts with long sleeves, a tight cuff and a frilled front – like Liberace used to wear! I asked one of the housekeepers to take care of it, and off she went, returning a few moments later, a puzzled look on her face. 'They're funny shirts, Mr Brennan. They weigh a ton for a start.'

'I'm sure they'll be fine,' I encouraged her. 'Just do your best.'

Off she went back to the ironing board, to emerge again a few minutes later, looking alarmed. 'Quick, Mr Brennan!' She ushered me into the ironing room and held up a shirt to me. 'Oh, God!' I exclaimed, because there, unavoidably, was a huge iron mark, right on the front of his shirt. 'Don't panic,' I said, calling our then-housekeeper, Miss O'Mahony, to come and survey the damage. It was her suggestion to cover the stain with Johnson's talcum powder, which we did, covering it liberally, then shaking it off. The stain could hardly be seen, we told ourselves, and without another word, we sent it and the other shirts back upstairs to Mr Coulter, and waited for the inevitable phone call. It never came! It would seem that our talcum powder fix had done the trick. I'm not sure I'd recommend it to you, but it saved our day.

I understand that nowadays we don't have time to press and starch sheets and tablecloths like Mum used to, and that we can fold T-shirts neatly to avoid having to iron them, but shirts really need to be ironed. I find that it's easiest when they are still slightly damp, or else the creases can be hard to get out.

Begin by selecting the correct temperature for the fabric of your shirt. Check the care label carefully. A cotton shirt can safely endure a high temperature, but cotton mix will need a lower one, and other fabrics, such as silk, will need the lowest temperature, with a covering of tissue paper for good measure.

- Turn the shirt inside out to iron the collars, cuffs and pockets, so that you don't get shine.

- I always iron the shoulders of my shirts next, pulling them onto the point of the board before ironing, then the back, before sliding to the front. I lay the sleeves out carefully on the board, cuffs open. Then I iron the cuffs, pulling them together gently, before pressing the rest of the sleeve, which I have placed flat on the ironing board, smoothing out the creases. If you don't want a crease in the middle of your sleeve, you'll need to move the sleeve around so that the crease is visible and iron it out.

- I always take care when I'm ironing around the buttons. I do it right side out, because I don't want shiny button shapes in the seam of my shirts.

Ironing is something that people either love or loathe. If you fall into the 'loathe' camp, you'll want to minimise the amount you do. Try hanging your clothes in the bathroom when you have a shower: the steam will remove any wrinkles. Also, fold or hang your clothes as soon as they come out of the drier to minimise the need for ironing. Think carefully about whether you really want to iron sheets, duvet covers or pillowcases – hanging them and then folding them carefully will result in smoother sheets.

If you love ironing, here are a few tips to improve your results:

- Stuff puffed sleeves with fabric or paper to make ironing easier.

- Put linen in the freezer for a few moments before ironing, for crispness.

- Iron silk on the lowest setting, through a layer of tissue paper.

- If you like freshly ironed sheets, double up on ironing by placing the sheet on the ironing board, then ironing your clothes as usual.

- Hang your clothes as soon as you've ironed them if you want to avoid ironing them again.

- Iron large things like sheets and duvet covers by folding them in two. When I get to the end of one side, I reverse the fold to reveal the creased side and set to again.

- Pleats are very hard to iron. Frankly, I prefer to leave them to the experts, but if you feel brave enough, the trick is to lay your skirt flat on the ironing board (only one layer on the board), then pull the bottom of the pleat gently until it's sitting flat. Pin with a paper clip or dressmaker's pin, then gently press. Repeat this all the way around your skirt until you get back to the beginning.

HOW TO ... REMOVE STAINS

Any queries about how to remove stains from upholstery and other surfaces always bring in a host of old wives' tales and suggestions. I love all of the different methods, from using potatoes to clean your windscreen to mayonnaise on wood stains! Some of the oldest remedies are indeed the best, such as using vinegar and newspaper to clean windows, but others are a bit fanciful. Here's my handy primer for some common fabric and surface stains:

Chocolate and chewing gum. Here's where the freezer comes into its own. Both substances are much easier to remove if you pop your jeans or cushion cover into the freezer. The gum or chocolate will harden and you can scrape it off. I've also discovered that milk can help to remove chocolate too, because it makes the fat in the chocolate break down. You soak your item in milk for half an hour, then wash as normal.

Strawberry/blackberry/other berry stains. Lemon juice is your friend here. Soak the offending stain in a solution of lemon juice, then wash and line dry.

Crayon. A cup of bread soda added to a hot wash will hopefully remove the offending crayon marks. Alternatively, hardening the crayon and scraping it off will work, and for larger stains, put the fabric between two pieces of kitchen paper and iron with a warm iron. The idea is that the crayon will come off onto the kitchen paper. If your lovely three-year-old has used crayon to do artwork on the walls, WD40, sprayed onto a cloth and wiped over the stain, will work wonders. Yes, WD40! A little dishwasher detergent applied after wipes off any oily residue. Old-fashioned white toothpaste smeared onto the stain and then wiped also works.

Mould. Every Irish household has mould. It's part and parcel of our damp climate. For some people, a solution of bleach is the only way to remove mould – or a cleaner containing bleach. This is certainly OK for bathrooms, but no one wants a house that smells of bleach! For clothing, you can add a cup of vinegar to a basin of water to pre-soak mouldy clothes or curtains, or upholstery that's safe to go in the washing machine. Borax is another thing that works really well on mouldy clothes: you can add it to the drum, or use a dilute solution, but follow the instructions on the packet. Finally, if you can't stand the smell of bleach, a dilute solution of one of those fizzy oxy cleaners is really good for stubborn mould in corners.

CHAPTER SIX

Waste Not,
Want Not

◇◇◇◇◇◇◇◇◇◇◇◇◇◇◇◇◇◇◇◇◇◇◇◇◇◇◇◇◇◇◇◇

'The earth does not belong to us.
We belong to the earth.'

CHIEF SEATTLE

Recycling is in the Brennan family blood, because we've been doing it for years without really realising, taking things up and down the road to Sligo. Our first recycling effort came with our much-loved TV, which came to our home in early 1962 – really something in those days, providing us with many hours' entertainment. So much so in fact that our homework began to suffer because we were always glued to the TV. So it was unplugged, packed into the back of the car and taken off to Sligo, never to be seen again!

Another time, we decided to bring a nice wardrobe that was too big for our Balally house up to Sligo, so it was duly fitted to the roof rack of the car and strapped down with rope, the decorative 'crown' left in the car. Somewhere between Mullingar and Longford, the wardrobe blew off in a gust of wind and smashed into umpteen pieces. We picked them up and tidied them behind the pillar of a farm gate, because we didn't know what else to do. To this day, every time I pass that farm, I have a laugh to myself.

So you can see that I've been a recycler for many years now, and of course at the hotel, we pay careful attention to recycling as much as possible. However, I'm new to the whole business of 'upcycling', which means reusing and repurposing what many of us might consider 'junk'. What is it they say, 'one man's junk is another man's treasure'?! I come from the generation where everything was reused and recycled, from the silver foil that my mother used to wash and use again to the shoes that were repaired time and time again. However, I also come from the generation where the concept of recycling as we now know it was unheard of. Everything, from batteries to lightbulbs, was thrown out in the bin. Thankfully, nowadays we know better. That doesn't mean that we act accordingly, but we know what we should aspire to.

A 2015 study found that Ireland ranked third in the EU for recycling, behind Slovenia, which recycles 55% of its waste, and Germany at 47%. Before we pat ourselves on the back too enthusiastically, though, it's worth mentioning that we were quite some way behind, at 34%. Still, that's progress from the dark days of the 1970s, when everything went to landfill. Taxation seems to have given us all a prod in the right direction, from the plastic bag levy to the landfill levy, and that's great, but apparently we need a little bit more incentive to compost our waste. We only compost about 6% of compostible waste, compared to the EU average of 15%. And we are a very long way behind some towns in America, like San Francisco and Berkeley, California, which recycle 70% of their waste. Then there is the leader of the pack, a little Japanese town called Kamikatsu, where there are no bin trucks – none! – and where 80% of waste is recycled, divided by the town's inhabitants into 34 separate categories and brought to a local centre, where a manager keeps a very careful eye on what they dump. Kamikatsu aims to be 'zero waste' by 2020 – surely something for us all to aspire to? If they can do it, so can we!

Now, I'm not mentioning all of these statistics to lecture you all. Like you, I could do more to help the environment in many ways, so I've done a little digging, if you'll excuse the pun, to help you make the most of your waste.

The Environmental Protection Agency Ireland (www.epa.ie) has a very useful 'portal' called 'livegreen', which has helpful hints for those of us who want to maximise recycling and reduce waste. Their top tips include:

- **Think before throwing anything away – can it be reused?**
- **Buy fruit and vegetables that have no unnecessary packaging.**
- **Make a shopping list and stick to it.**
- **Look for non-hazardous alternatives for cleaning at home. Safer substitutes, like vinegar, lemon juice, baking soda, salt and olive oil used alone or in various combinations can get the job done!**

FOOD WASTE

I'm feeling pretty pleased with myself, because I've spent most of this book going on about vinegar, baking soda and lemon juice! However, some of the information about food waste made me sit up and pay attention. Working in a hotel, we are very conscious of food waste – when we buy food, when we cook it and when it returns to the kitchen. I also come from a generation when food was eaten fresh and the days of the week were entirely predictable, food wise. We always ate our main meal in the middle of the day, and we always ate the same food. In our house, Monday was the 'lonely dinner', as John used to call it, which was Sunday's leftover roast, eaten with a slick of gravy over it; Tuesday was stew; Wednesday, bacon and cabbage; Thursday was lamb's liver, because the butcher would have killed the lambs the day before so it would be fresh; Friday was fish always, generally plaice or cod; Saturday, Mum might do a delicious stuffed pork steak; and Sunday was a roast, lamb or beef, but almost never chicken. We Brennan's ate very well, by the standards of the time, but chicken was a luxury then. We'd only eat chicken at our friends the Redmonds' caravan in Donabate on Monday afternoons, when Dad's shop would be shut – remember when shops used to close for a half-day?! A whole chicken would do all of us, Brennans plus Redmonds!

So, in the spirit of times past, the first step in reducing your food waste is to plan ahead. Rather than visiting the supermarket every time you feel hungry, grabbing random items off the shelf, write a good-old-fashioned shopping list. Look into your larder, fridge and freezer and see what you have – you'd be surprised at what's lurking at the back of your cupboards! Then make a list: I always plan my shopping around meals that I'm going to have during the week. So if I've decided on spaghetti bolognese or a nice roast, my mind is automatically calculating how I can get the most out of my meat – mince can double up for the spaghetti sauce and as the basis for a shepherd's pie. I can roast a chicken and use any leftovers in a pie or stir-fry, or cold in a salad or a lovely chicken sandwich.

Vegetables pose a particular challenge when shopping. I don't know about you, but I'm inclined to be tempted by special offers on fruit and veg – buy one get one free, that kind of thing, or at a very low price. Resist! If you buy a kilo of parsnips, are you really going to use them all, or will they end up being thrown out? After a few impulse buys, I've certainly learned my lesson. Special offers are great for things like washing powder or toiletries, but when it comes to food, I let temptation pass me by! Again, I try to buy veg according to the meals I'm planning, rather than the deals on offer. It's interesting to note that some of the supermarket chains have changed their mind about special offers on fruit and veg, and they now encourage us all just to buy what we need. The same goes for discounted food which is close to its expiry date: it's only a bargain if you are actually going to eat it! Avoid buying unless you plan to eat it that day, or to freeze it.

Which brings me to another food waste issue. Have you ever rummaged around in your freezer and found a lot of tubs and bags full of leftover food? You lift it out and have a look at it, and you can't for the life of you remember (a) what it is and (b) when you put it there! In the spirit of full disclosure, a look in my own freezer revealed two big cuts of ham, leftovers from Christmas, two tubs of what looked like spaghetti sauce and a large amount of frozen bread – I'm a great believer in freezing bread because when defrosted, it's nice and fresh – but my freezer drawers are full of bits of sourdough! It's time for some freezer discipline:

- **Label everything you put into your freezer so that you know how long you have to eat it.**
- **Check food labels to see how long food can be frozen.**
- **Make sure to place most recent items at the back of the freezer so that you'll take older items out first – great advice from www.stopfoodwaste.ie.**

- Clear out your freezer every three months or so. Resolve that you'll use up everything in the freezer that week and plan your meals around that – so I'll be eating a lot of ham for a while!

- I put food into freezer bags, because they take up less room in the freezer and leave my nice plastic containers free.

- Make sure to defrost your freezer regularly so that it works efficiently.

The www.stopfoodwaste.ie website also lists a number of foods that you might not have realised can be frozen. Very handy – but remember to check carefully how to defrost these foods safely. Certain foods, like cooked rice, can give you nasty bugs if you don't follow the rules about reheating, so always, always check.

For your information, you can freeze:

- Cheese – yes, really! If you seal the bag well, cheese can keep for up to six months.

- Cold processed meats.

- Nuts.

- Whole eggs – which can be beaten and then frozen for instant omelettes.

- Fruit – such as berries, which freeze easily, bananas (a great way of preventing them from going brown), cherries, melon etc.

- Milk – great if you live a while away from the shops and need it in an emergency.

- Wine – although why you'd want to freeze it is beyond me. I suppose you could do so for use in risottos and stews. I'm not a drinker, but I still think I'd prefer something nice in a bottle!

Foods that don't freeze well are:

- Anything with egg white in it – meringues, cooked egg whites, icing with egg white in it – all go 'tough, rubbery, spongy' according to the US National Center for Food Preservation (NCFP).

- Cream or custard fillings or milk-based sauces, like béchamel. They will split upon freezing.

- Fried foods 'lose crispness, become soggy' according to the NCFP.

- Mayonnaise or salad cream.

- Cabbage, lettuce, cucumber – all become mushy and soggy.

- Cooked pasta – which goes mushy and tastes spongy.

- Spicy foods can also lose their oomph when frozen – spices are really best added fresh to curries or spicy stews. My advice would be to freeze your stew base without spices and add them to the defrosted base, so you'll have a nice fresh taste. Curries often taste great when left for a day or two in the fridge – but I'd be inclined to eat them then, rather than freezing, for maximum taste.

If you want to avoid food waste, check www.stopfoodwaste.ie for other handy hints; I particularly liked their January 'eat what you have' challenge, which can be applied to any time of the year. If you feel that the cupboards are bare and you need to do a shop, stop. Open the cupboards, fridge and freezer and have a good look. I'll bet you'll find a few days' worth of frozen fruit, veg, sauces, stews and plenty of tins of tomatoes or pulses. This might not please the non-vegetarians among us, but we're all supposed to be eating less meat anyway! Make it a resolution to shop only when your cupboards and freezer are bare. Many people find that shopping little and often also helps – keeping a store of basics at home and then adding fresh foods to these daily, but it does require discipline and wouldn't suit the impulse shoppers among us. However, if you are trying to beat food waste, this can really work.

CATHY'S TIP:

Did you know that you can freeze butter? It saves it from going off if you don't use it very often. Keep your butter well wrapped to prevent it being tainted by other fridge smells.

If you have limp vegetables or fruit lurking in your crisper drawer, all is not lost. You can easily refresh old veg by giving them a good dunk in olive oil, salt and pepper and roasting them. You can also stew old fruit, freezing portions for use in porridge and breakfast yoghurts. Leftovers – if used properly – can be the basis of lots of lovely meals. If, like me, you store leftovers in the fridge, check it regularly – many's the time I have come across something mouldy in my fridge that I put there, covered and completely forgot about!

Because I travel a lot and am not home much, I don't 'do' leftovers, but I know that they can be a lifesaver for busy families. Here are a few tips for using leftovers:

- **Use leftover dinners for lunch the next day. Cathy will often turn cold pasta into a salad, with a bit of pesto and some chopped chicken, or she'll pop some chilli (meat or veg) into a wrap with a grating of cheese for lunch.**

- **Stale white bread can become bread-and-butter pudding or the basis of an Italian 'bread' salad called panzanella – lovely in the summer with fresh tomatoes and basil. It can also be blitzed in the food processor as breadcrumbs (which can be frozen), or toasted under the grill with a drizzle of good olive oil – the uses are endless!**

- **If you are making pasta sauce, always make double and freeze the rest. Cathy uses plain tomato sauces for pasta toppings, but also for pizza. A great way to use up fridge leftovers is to buy ready-made pizza bases, pop some tomato sauce onto them, and then use up those stray slices of ham, that half jar of olives, the old bit of Parmesan, etc.**

- **If you spot a bargain 1kg packet of mince, buy it by all means, but divide it into two or four portions, depending on your family size – use one and freeze the rest. Or, make a giant portion of bolognese sauce and freeze half of it.**

- **Remember the Sunday roast that would do for Monday and Tuesday too? Get into the habit of making your food work for you by thinking of how many meals you can get out of it. For example, that ham I have lurking in my freezer could be roasted, the leftovers fried with potatoes** and cabbage to make an Irish bubble and squeak; put into a ham pie; or used to make a lovely ham sandwich, and so on. My point is, make your food stretch.

- Vegetables can be reused in soups – a basic vegetable soup, with a softened onion and veg, followed by some stock, can be adapted to use up any amount of the veg you find in your fridge.

- You can add your leftover meat to pasta and smother it in a creamy sauce, then pop on some breadcrumbs and into the oven it goes.

- Don't forget that you can use cold meat in a nice salad too.

- Frittatas and tortillas are brilliant ways to use up leftover vegetables. A frittata is a kind of omelette into which you can put just about anything, before popping into the oven; a tortilla is the stove-top version. And don't forget quiches – another use for my ham!

- Rice is particularly good reheated in Chinese fried rice or a paella, but please do remember to reheat it properly. If you make more rice than you need, cool it quickly (otherwise bacteria might multiply), put it into the fridge and eat the next day – no later. Cook it until it is piping hot throughout: this is particularly important with rice.

- Cool all food properly before storing it in the fridge. If you are not freezing, make sure to eat any leftovers within 48 hours. Heat all leftovers thoroughly and don't reheat more than once.

CATHY'S TIP:

Put a slice or two of apple in the jar with your brown sugar. The moisture will stop it caking into a big clump.

THE BIN

No matter how careful you are with food waste or with packaging, of course you'll have a kitchen bin – and it will get filled with food and other kinds of waste, particularly food packaging. Packaging is the bugbear of many of us. It seems that we simply can't get away from it. It smothers every product, it's hard to open and awful things like plastic cable ties require sharp tools to remove. What's more, it has led to the phenomenon of 'wrap rage', where people get frustrated not being able to open the packaging!

Clear plastic dominates packaging because it's cheap and because it displays whatever is inside it; worse in my view is polystyrene. I am sorry to say that I unwittingly bought a package of apples the other week, to discover that they came in a polystyrene tray. As this can't be recycled, into the landfill it goes.

I have noticed a bin behind the till in some supermarkets, filled with the customers' packaging. What a great idea, I thought. However, before you go marching into your local supermarket to demand they take your frozen pizza boxes, note that if they are members of REPAK, they already pay membership fees, which allows councils to remove, sort and recycle packaging, so they are not obliged to take yours. Know that your packaging will end up in the recycling anyway if you sort it carefully, separating any plastic interiors from cardboard exteriors.

Unfortunately, increasing waste charges have led some of us to be very cavalier about what goes into our recycling bins: to our shame, in 2017, it was estimated that 40% of 'green bin' waste was not actually recyclables, because many people were putting 'black bin' waste into the green bins to avoid charges. And some of that waste was hazardous, to say the least. It's not up to me to lecture, but just remember, real human beings have to sort your recycling, so be aware of this when you are putting things into your green bin.

REPAK (www.repak.ie) lists the following as 'contaminants', which should not go in the green bin:

- Nappies and sanitary products (including baby wipes).
- Food waste.
- Contaminated packaging.
- Garden cuttings or soil.
- Polystyrene (EPS).
- Liquids or oils.
- Textiles – including clothes/shoes and home furnishings.
- Dismantled furniture.
- Medical waste.
- Glass.
- Light bulbs.
- Electrical and electronic equipment, i.e. anything that can contain a battery or a plug.
- Batteries.
- General waste that should be in the general waste bin.

While these are the things your green bin can take:

- Paper, including newspapers, catalogues, junk mail, computer paper, phone books, tissue boxes etc.
- Cardboard – including cereal and packaging boxes, as well as food boxes (with any interior plastic removed).
- Plastic – including shampoo, detergent and soap bottles – well rinsed – and plastic fruit packaging with the netting removed. Plastic netting is also recyclable, but needs to be separated from the box.
- Cans/tins – both steel and aluminium, so food cans and also biscuit tins – remember to take the plastic inserts out first.

- **Metal lids from jam or sauce jars. Yes, you can include these with your recycling, but just make sure they're clean.**

- **Plastic bags can also be recycled, but again, make sure that you've cleaned them before putting them in the recycling.**

For those of you who live outside the big cities, finding your nearest bring centre or recycling depot can be more of a challenge, but if you feel that recycling is a bit of a waste of time, a few statistics from REPAK will give you some encouragement to keep up the good work! Did you know, for example, that plastic is made from crude oil, which is non-renewable, so it makes all the more sense to recycle it. Also of interest is the fact that in Europe our use of plastic is actually growing, not declining. But if we recycle, we can use up to two-thirds less energy than we'd use in making plastic from raw materials – good news and a big incentive to recycle. And if that weren't enough, did you know that a discarded plastic bag can stay in the ground for up to 500 years? I don't want to frighten you here, but we all need a little nudge in the right direction, including myself.

If you want to recycle bigger appliances, like toasters, kettles, washing machines etc., the WEEE initiative is a great thing. It's basically a compliance scheme on behalf of organisations and companies that produce electrical equipment. That's why, when you buy a new washing machine, the store will take back your old one and recycle it, either when they deliver the new machine or at an agreed date. Here's what WEEE Ireland has to say: 'If you give your customer a 24-hour notice of delivery and the product is prepared for collection you must offer take back on delivery. If the product is not prepared the customer can still return it indefinitely to your store. If you do not give a 24-hour notice of delivery then the customer can ask you to return and take it back within 15 days.'

So now you know! WEEE members are obliged to take back appliances on a 'one for one' basis, but larger members (with floor space of greater than $400m^2$) are also obliged to take back small electrical appliances without you having to buy anything in return – surely great news!

You can also recycle small or large electrical appliances and pesky batteries, which are so hard to get rid of, not to mention unsafe if left to leak – just bring them to your nearest recycling centre, which will have a WEEE facility. And if you live in the country at some distance from your nearest recycling centre, collection days are organised – just check on the website, www.weeeireland.ie. It's a great excuse to clear out your attic or garage and get rid of old electrical equipment.

COMPOSTING

One of the great ways to use up certain types of household waste is to compost it, and this reminds me once more of our handyman at home in Balally. His antics left us with a fund of stories. I recall that he came from the midlands somewhere – it may have been County Offaly – and he used to return home every now and again on his bicycle. Now, he used to do some work for the nuns while he was down at home, and they had a farm, and he'd fill up two buckets of nice hot manure and he'd go up the town to his own house, steam wafting from the buckets! He used to put the manure on his own roses and, indeed, they were lovely. 'Well, you can't beat the nuns' sh*te', as he used to say, whenever he'd get a compliment about them!

Now, while most of us won't have manure to hand – blessed or not – we can put green leaves, prunings, eggshells, old teabags, coffee grounds, vegetable peelings, cardboard and untreated paper into the compost bin or heap, as well as shredded natural fibres like cotton or linen. You can also put in the droppings from your hamster, rabbit or bird cage, which is very useful for those of us who have little furries, as well as manure from cows or horses, fantastic if you have larger livestock. However, you can't put cat or dog poo onto your compost heap or into your bin, because of the risk of disease. The same goes for unhealthy plants or clippings and anything organic that has attracted flies. As a rule, you *can't* put fish, meat or dairy products into your compost bin, because they will attract more than just flies! If you want to avoid visits from not-so-nice furry friends or other pests, don't put them into your bin. I say, 'as a rule', because some newer systems actually allow you to put all food waste into your bin, but more on that later.

If you are new to composting, you can either build your own home composter – all you need is a contained space to hold the compost, or you can buy a compost bin – many local authorities sell them at reduced prices, so go online and check yours out to see if they offer them. The main tips are to mix your 'green' (clippings, grass, leaves etc.) with your 'brown' (peelings, teabags etc.) and to break the piles up with little twigs and bits of straw to allow air to circulate. This helps everything to break down.

Some of you with larger gardens might have seen one of those green 'tumblers' on legs, with a little hatch at the top. In this system, you throw in a whole batch of collected brown and green waste and turn it in the tumbler every few days. It does require quite a lot of supervision, but it makes compost more quickly – might be good for the avid gardener!

Food digesters are another form of composter – the professional ones are a kind of green cone that is placed half over and half under the soil, and is filled with food waste. The sun then turns this into compost, which sinks down under the ground – brilliant! And for those of you dying to get rid of dog and cat poo, this is for you, as the digester will process both, as well as fish and meat scraps. DIY-ers among you will be glad to know that you can make your own food digester by drilling holes in the bottom of an ordinary garden bin – a metal one – and sinking the holed part down under the soil. The beauty of this is that worms will find their way up through the holes and help your compost to break down. Clearly it's not for a balcony, though, so not ideal if you have little space.

If space is at a premium, you might like to try a *wormery*, which can be shop bought or even home-made. The shop-bought ones are great for beginners, as they are a ready-made system with a solid bin, a tap for the 'liquid' that is produced, and even a bag of worms! These aren't earthworms, by the way, but 'tiger' worms, which are great compost makers.

Getting your wormery started is easy: you just place a layer of bedding at the bottom – usually coir, which should be supplied along with the wormery – it's like a worm sleeping bag! Then you add the worms and finally a layer of peelings/leaves and shredded newspaper at the bottom and let the worms munch away. It isn't the easiest of systems, though, because you have to keep an eye on your worms. If you notice that your waste isn't being munched, you might have put too much in for their little worm stomachs! Make sure that you chop it up small and only add small amounts to give them time to work. And don't let them get too cold or too hot. Another tip for wormeries is to remember to drain off the excess water with the little tap. If you are an avid gardener with a big space, a wormery may not be for you, but it is ideal for those of us with small spaces who want to get rid of waste. They even do wormeries for pet poo!

Our friends at www.stopfoodwaste.ie have a handy downloadable composting guide full of tips and information on home composting.

HOUSEHOLD BUDGETS

While we're on the subject of 'waste', now seems a good time to talk about how we spend money. This is a tricky subject, because everyone has his or her own ideas about spending and saving and I'm not one to lecture anyone, but it's also true to say that we could all do with a few lessons in how not to waste this most valuable resource – myself included! It's also good to teach children the finer points of household budgeting, because it will prepare them for life.

Having said that, my mum and dad were not big budgeters, to be honest. They believed in having the best of everything – in particular, putting a good-quality dinner on the table every night. There's nothing at all wrong with that, because they weren't big spenders in lots of other ways. Each of us cuts our cloth to suit our measure. However, if you get to the end of the month with nothing in your bank account or find that credit is causing you to overspend, think about having a household budget. You might be pleasantly surprised at how much money you actually have, once you organise things a little bit.

There are lots of budgeting tools online, including a number of free downloadable spreadsheets, but the one I like best is from the Money Advice and Budgeting Service – MABS (www.mabs.ie). It only takes 20 minutes, so it's ideal for busy people. You'll need some utility bills, your payslip and your weekly shopping bill to hand, but you can calculate your budget weekly or monthly, and it has ideas on increasing your income and decreasing your outgoings, including a little spending diary. You don't have to write an entire year's worth of expenditure into it, just track your spending for a couple of weeks or so – this will give you a good idea about how you spend your money and on what.

Of course, there is a difference between spending and wasting money. All of us need to spend money, but sometimes we spend more than we need to, and not just on impulse buys, but also on things that we might consider essential, like insurance.

WASTING MONEY

I love this heading, because I could do with some reminders myself in how to spend money wisely. Look first at your weekly shop, as this is the one thing you simply can't cut out. I won't lecture you all on own brands and cheaper cuts of meat, because you will all have your own standards on that kind of thing, but a few general tips are helpful:

- **Don't shop on an empty stomach – this might sound obvious, but have you ever gone around the supermarket before dinner? Your stomach** is rumbling and before you know it you find yourself reaching for chocolate biscuits and all kinds of things that you'd normally ignore. Eat before you go and avoid buying more than you need. Another great tip is to limit your time in the supermarket. If you only have 20 minutes, you won't have time to browse – instead, you can follow that shopping list you wrote before you left the house.

- Do the grocery shopping by yourself if you possibly can. Those of you with children will know that shopping with them is a sure-fire way of adding impulse purchases to your trolley, even just to keep them quiet! Hiring a babysitter might sound like a complete extravagance, but you might find that you actually save money if you don't have the kids loading the basket with extras. Can you swap children with a friend, to allow each of you to do the weekly grocery shop in peace?

- I remember seeing a TV financial advice expert suggesting that people put their credit card in the freezer to avoid being tempted to take it out and spend with it! If this sounds a bit drastic, why not simply nominate one day of the week as a 'no-spending' day and see if you can leave your purse at home? You might find that you go for a walk and bring a sandwich at lunchtime instead of buying one at the deli counter, which is good, but it's really all about getting into the discipline of not spending if you don't need to. It's a bit like giving something up for Lent – once you get used to doing without sugar in your tea, you become a bit of a convert!

- Don't go overboard with cleaning products. If you look at the supermarket aisle, you'll see a cleaning product for every possible type of surface and cleaning job – but all of those wipes and sprays come at a cost. I've been preaching the gospel of old-fashioned cleaning products in this book, and there's one other great thing about them: because you can use them in a lot of different ways, they could save you money.

- Convenience shopping is an easy way to spend more money than you should. Instead of buying that bottle of water at the shop, buy a 12-pack at the supermarket. Of course, you'll want to go to the newsagent's to buy the paper and the Lotto ticket, but perhaps buy expensive items, like drinks and food, from cheaper outlets.

- Look at your TV subscription to see if you can save money. Many suppliers have 'bundles' that include TV and broadband, but with so many alternatives to TV, including free 'player' services, check if you really need the monthly subscription, or if another supplier offers it more cheaply – or indeed if a streaming service is all you need. There are also the 'one-off' deals, where you buy a set-top box for a one-off fee for the main channels – which, let's face it, are probably the ones you use most.

- Look out for budget plans on energy bills. My friend Cathy used to dread the massive energy bills that would drop on her doormat after a chilly winter – after the Big Freeze a few years ago, they had an office competition to see who had the highest bill! Cathy solved her post-winter fright by switching to a monthly budget plan. Now, she knows how much she'll have to pay each month. And even if you don't have a budget plan, always submit your meter reading, as otherwise you might be paying an 'estimated' reading. Of course, it all balances out, but it will save unwelcome surprises!

- I don't know about you, but I've found the arrival of contactless payments on my debit cards a bit of a mixed blessing. It's convenient, but I'm inclined to pay for things without even noticing. If budgeting is an issue for you, try removing a fixed amount of cash from your account every week and just spending that.

- Bargains are only bargains if you really need the item. There's no point in paying for a 'bogof' (buy one get one free) in a breakfast cereal you don't eat, or shampoo you don't use. You won't save any money on things that you didn't need to buy in the first place. The same goes for clothes. It makes sense to buy a winter coat at the end of the season, when it's cheap, and keep it for next winter, but it makes less sense to buy lots of cheap clothes instead of a smaller number of quality items. I believe that fast fashion has a lot to answer for, in terms of sustainability and ethics, so try to be a bit more conscious of what you really need. I think a great tip is to ask yourself, 'Do I need this or do I just want it?' That generally sorts the wheat from the chaff!

- Look at insurance carefully. Needless to say, we all need to insure our homes and cars, but what about other kinds of insurance? Have you ever been offered insurance for your mobile phone? Look at the small print and check that it's good value for money. Some insurance products have lots of exclusions and might not be worth the purchase price. Similarly, many people swear by pet insurance, because vets' fees can really add up these days, but, again, look at the plans carefully, to make sure that everything you need is covered and examine clauses relating to pre-existing conditions and excesses closely, as they vary from insurer to insurer. You might also find that certain breeds are more expensive to insure, and some breeds considered to be dangerous may not even be insurable. If you are paying for pet insurance, shop around. A good tip is to insure your pet young, as you will get the most out of your policy.

- Travel insurance is something that people think essential – and of course, you'll want to make sure that you are covered for accidents, illnesses and theft abroad – but like everything else, it pays to shop around. For a start, look at other policies you might have. I recently discovered that my health insurance policy also covers me for travel insurance – all I needed to do was to register and, hey presto, I was covered! Some of you might find that your private health insurance also covers you for travel, or at least will get you a discount, so don't be afraid to ask.

- For travel insurance generally an annual 'multi-trip' policy is cheaper than, say, insuring one trip, but this depends on how often you travel. Unfortunately, age can't be avoided when it comes to travel insurance. If you are older – over 50 – you'll generally have to pay more, and there's no way of getting around it. You might be charged more for 'multi-trip' insurance, or indeed find that the insurer won't offer you a policy at all. But some insurers continue to offer insurance to older people, and indeed some cater specifically for the oldies, with policies for those aged 65 and over. Look at the excess clause carefully – it does differ between insurers – and check if they exclude those with pre-existing conditions. Don't be tempted to tell fibs if you have an illness, though, as it might affect you later. Remember, if you are travelling within the EU, you can avail of public health care if you get a European Health Insurance Card (EHIC) – some of you might remember this as the old E111. You can apply for the EHIC card at your local health office, and the form is downloadable from the HSE website. If you already have a card, or indeed have a medical card or Drugs Payment Scheme card, all you have to do is to renew your EHIC card online.

- Cut the coffee habit. I'm not a coffee drinker, but I have a friend who loves his lattes, and buys two a day. That's €5.80. Multiply that by, say, six days a week, and you are looking at a very expensive habit! By all means treat yourself to a coffee every now and again, but try not to make it a regular thing if you are looking to save money. As for cigarettes, I won't even go there, because the smokers among you are well aware of the cost of it, I'm sure – and not just the financial one.

- Make sure that you are claiming all of the benefits or tax breaks that you're entitled to. Don't forget that you can claim for 'out of the ordinary' dental expenses, like crowns, root-canal treatment and orthodontics etc., on the form MED2 with the Revenue. If you are doing up your home, you might also be entitled to a tax break, and the same if you have a pension. If you are on a lower income, check your entitlements to benefits with your local benefits office, to make sure that you are not missing out on anything you are entitled to.

- Claim your benefits on loyalty cards. Many of us sign up to store loyalty cards, but check to see which ones have the best benefits before clogging up your wallet with cards. And don't forget to claim them! You might be surprised at how much you've built up and you can then treat yourself to a little spending spree with your bonus points.

REPAIRS

Do you remember when we used to repair everything, when there was a shop in every town and village that did appliance repairs, fixing everything from TVs to vacuum cleaners to washing machines and so on? I think you'd be hard pressed to find a 'little man' nowadays to fix your broken TV set! This makes it much more likely that we'll throw out appliances that break down. Added to this we'll often find that, because 'white goods' are so much cheaper nowadays, the cost of repairs often outweighs that of buying a new appliance.

The Swedish government has taken a novel and forward-looking approach (trust the Scandinavians to be ahead of the pack!): cutting VAT on repairs. It's also proposing a tax cut for people who get repairs done on appliances. There's nothing like a financial incentive to encourage us to get repairs done. Of course, you can avoid repairs if you look after your appliances carefully:

- Get them serviced regularly – this might seem expensive, but it's not half as expensive as having to replace your boiler or washing machine!

- Check things like smoke detectors, carbon monoxide monitors and fire extinguishers to make sure that the battery is fresh and that all of the parts are working.

- Bleed radiators once a year. You'll know that there is trapped air in your radiators if the whole radiator isn't warm. If you have turned the boiler on, switch it off again and wait until it cools down. Then find the 'bleed valve' on your radiator. If you haven't a clue what a bleed valve is, let alone where to find it, it is on the side of your radiator, either at the top or bottom – depending on the style of your radiator – and it's a sort of hexagonal bolt, onto which you fit a little key that looks like one you would use to wind up a clock. If you don't have a key, your DIY store will have one. Put a bit of old sheet underneath the valve and make sure that your hand is well covered, as sometimes what comes out can be hot. Turn your key anticlockwise and prepare for a hissing sound, followed by a trickle of water – this is normal. The trickle tells you that the air has been let out of your radiator, so you can turn the key back again. There you go – one device that you can master without needing the help of a plumber! Needless to say, if there is any problem that you don't know how to solve – get a plumber. Some repairs are not for the faint-hearted, so, if in doubt, don't do it yourself.

- Keep your washing machine and dishwasher clean by running them empty with a hot wash once in a while. Use rinse aid in your dishwasher and clean the filter regularly so that it doesn't get clogged. You can find handy tablets to clean your washing machine as well these days – pop one into the detergent drawer to keep your machine clean and free of hard deposits. Also, keep the rubbery rim around the door clean, as it can really smell horrible, and remove and clean the detergent drawer every now and again. This maintenance is easily done and could save you having to call out an expert. However, when it comes to your fridge, be careful. Don't attempt anything beyond cleaning regularly and perhaps keeping the element dust free – fridges are best left to the experts.

- If you have one of the newer types of freezer, you won't even need to defrost it, but if you have an older type, remember that it will work more efficiently if you defrost it every three months or so. You'll need to remove all of the freezer contents – so perhaps have a freezer-food week before you do so, to use up the frozen food – and you'll need to unplug and let the ice melt, catching the (considerable) puddles of water in a basin placed on tea towels. And don't do what I once did and go out only to come home and find a giant puddle of water in the kitchen! Defrost your freezer when you know you'll be around for the afternoon. Did you know that while your fridge doesn't have to be full to work well, it really helps if your freezer is – all those frozen bags of peas help to keep the freezer temperature as low as possible.

- The one thing you really need to do with your dryer is clean the lint tray every time you use it. Believe me, lint builds up very quickly and it can be a fire hazard, so check that lint tray every time you want to use the machine. Also, once a year, check the pipe that goes from the machine to the outside for lint build-up. You might need to hoover lint out before reattaching the pipe.

- Keep your cooker clean, whether it's gas or electric. Some of you lucky readers will have a self-cleaning oven, but it does use a lot of energy; if you don't, you can make your own oven cleaner using half a lemon with sugar sprinkled onto it – it's a lovely, natural-smelling oven cleaner and a tonic after those strong-smelling commercial cleaners. Make sure that your gas burners are working efficiently by keeping them clean and free of food spills. I can still remember our old gas oven blowing up when I was a teenager. Mum turned on the oven by accident, without remembering to light the pilot light and the oven door blew off – and yes, while gas is a lot safer nowadays, it pays to take no chances.

UPCYCLING

When my parents brought their brand-new home in Balally in 1951, they didn't have a stick of furniture. Instead, Dad brought a few Jaffa orange boxes home from the shop to use as chairs, and Mum and Dad sat on them for a full year before being able to afford chairs. It didn't matter, of course, because every young couple did the same in those days. Furniture was expensive and you had to save up for it, which they did, adding to their collection every year and taking one room at a time. They inherited bits and pieces from relatives, including the beautiful table that my grandfather made, which I now have, and elaborate 'overmantel' mirrors – mirrors with lovely mahogany inlay that sat over the mantelpiece and are still around today. Mum and Dad were upcyclers before their time!

From furniture to shipping containers, upcycling is such a buzz word at the moment – what exactly does it mean? Well, before you throw out that set of bookshelves or the pallet that your washing machine arrived on, or indeed, an old dining-room table that won't fit in your modern home, ask yourself a few questions:

- **Could I find another use for this item?** No, you probably can't repurpose your old toaster, so it will need to be recycled, but you might be able to find a new use for the wine rack you were about to throw out – all you need is a little bit of inspiration.

- **Can I repair it?** Sometimes an object can easily be fixed, or you can find a new use for it, but other times you just won't have the expertise, so, again, it's time to recycle.

- **Will it take more time and energy to fix than to replace?** The $64 million question! Many people get very excited when they see an old chair or a broken table: they know exactly what to do to breathe new life into it, but they quickly grow frustrated at the sheer amount of time and effort involved in this difficult DIY project. Be kind to yourself – only fix things if you really have the time and energy to do so.

- Is it structurally sound? There's no point in making a sofa out of an old bed if it collapses the minute you sit on it! If there are any cracks that can't be repaired, be safe and dispose of the item. Mattresses pose particular problems, because they used to end up in landfills. However, a couple of social enterprise organisations now recycle them, and organise collections from businesses and individuals for a fee, but sadly only in Cork and Dublin to date. The same goes for your old bicycle, which will go to a charity that restores old bikes and sells them on, and indeed old furniture as well, also recyclable via a social enterprise group. Unfortunately, these services aren't available countrywide, but as one recycling supplier noted, recycling companies are like any other: they are businesses, and there has to be a market for what they are offering, so it pays to buy items that have been recycled, fully or partly, to do your bit to make this market more competitive. Hopefully, one day everything we buy will have been recycled, but that's a long way away – in the meantime, do what you can.

There are a couple of organisations that bring together keen upcyclers, and a quick glance reveals all kinds of objects that have found a new use: a wine glass and fruit bowl made out of old keys, which had been cleverly soldered together – don't try this at home! – a coffee table made out of old wine crates, and a clever key holder made out of old doorknobs. I saw lovely hand-made paper flowers, made out of all kinds of paper; handbags made out of old sails, believe it or not; soft toys made out of old fabric; furniture made out of old boxes or pallets; a bench made out of an unwanted bunk bed – the list of 'repurposed' old things is endless. However, there's no doubting that you have to be fairly handy at DIY to do some of them – I don't think I'll be attempting to make key sculptures any time soon! Be enthusiastic, but also be realistic about what you can reuse and repurpose.

I remember that Mum used to make stools, for some reason – something to do with a home for the blind. She used to get raffia and a steel frame, I recall, and she'd weave the stool seat, then attach them to the frame. We had three or four, and they made great places to put a tray or your feet. Some upcycling projects are lovely and easy, but I've also seen furniture ideas that have turned into fairly labour-intensive projects. A friend of mine recently tried to upcycle an old gramophone cabinet, which had actually been repurposed by her grandfather many years before into a cocktail cabinet. She set to, before realising that the whole thing was riddled with woodworm! Her project involved quite a painstaking process of treating the wood, sanding it down, painting it and so on. Upcycling is terrific, but it does involve energy and time. Easier, perhaps, is upcycling fabrics – using the fabric from an old dress to make a nice bag or cushion cover, finding a pattern to make a cuddly toy out of old fabric. I saw an innovative use for an old cardboard box – the kind we all get our deliveries in nowadays, wrapped in jute string (using a hot glue gun, so be careful!) and with a liner tucked inside – hey presto, a handy and attractive storage box!

Coffee cans can be painted and used for all kinds of things, from plant pots to pencil holders. Wooden clothes hangers (the kind that snap together to hold trousers) make genuinely nice picture holders – really! Screw-top jars are also great, because they can be decorated easily and will hold anything, from rice to pulses. And you don't even have to be handy to repurpose an old tin can with little holes (push a nail through), paint it and put a tea light into it. You can get the kids to cover tissue boxes with decorative paper and use them as pencil tidies. I even saw a knife block very cleverly transformed into a lovely art station and a vacuum cleaner hose transformed into a wreath! Wooden crates are really handy for all kinds of storage, and you can even fix one to your bicycle back carrier with cable ties to carry the shopping. Once you get started thinking this way, you'll find that you can't stop.

If you think that upcycling doesn't fit into your busy lifestyle, think of what you can do to support people who do upcycle, many of whom are members of social enterprise schemes: you can donate anything from bedding to sofas to other items on various 'freecycling' websites (www.freetradeireland.ie); you can even organise collections of unwanted items via your residents' association – the Community Reuse Network Ireland is a good place to start for organisations in this area – www.crni ie.

I came across one innovative Irish charity that will take your unwanted old computer, which will be renewed and repaired and find its way to the developing world (www.camara.org), and plenty of social enterprise schemes that urge businesses to recycle and offer for exchange everything from light fittings to old desks (www.smileexchange.ie). It is true that many upcycling and freecycling initiatives are Dublin-based, but the freecycling movement (www.freecycle.org) has a list of all of the community schemes in the country, so you will be able to find one near you. If there isn't one, why not set one up yourself?

All of us can recycle and upcycle. The only thing you need to do is check before you dump to see if your item can be recycled or reused elsewhere. And remember the basic concept of upcycling, an old-fashioned concept – make do and mend – that has found a new lease of life in the 21st century.

HOW TO ... DO SOME EASY HOME UPCYCLING

Old pillowcases can make great garment bags – in fact, the fabric is ideally suited to storing your clothes, so why not give it a try? Take the closed end of your pillowcase and make a 4cm or so slit in the seam. You can do this by turning the pillowcase inside out and unpicking a few of the stitches in the middle. Get out your needle and thread and make a little stitch on either side of the slit to make sure that the seam doesn't unravel further. Turn your pillowcase out, slide the hanger in and – you have a garment bag!

I found a sweet **little fabric bookmark** that would use up old fabric scraps – and it actually looked very handy into the bargain! All you need are your fabric scraps and a piece of narrow elastic – about 1cm wide. If you are making a bookmark for a standard paperback, this will be around 15cm long, so cut two 15 x 6 cm strips of fabric. At this point, the tidier among you might like to hem the strips by turning down a half centimetre edge top and bottom and hemming – or if you are feeling lazy, placing a piece of fabric webbing under each hem and ironing. Next, place the two strips together, right side down, then sew along the edges of the strips. Don't sew along the short edge yet. Turn this tube of fabric right side out, then give it a little iron. Now you need to attach your elastic to the bottom edge of each end of the tube, and you have a bookmark!

I also came across a DIY project that invited me to make ties for a three-month-old baby, which amused me no end. I could turn him into a mini Francis! A little more practical would be **upcycling old T-shirts**. All you need to do is to remove the sleeves below the seams, then cut an opening for your bag by placing a dinner plate upside down about 5cm below the neck opening. Mark a line and then cut it to form a larger opening for your bag. Now, all you need to do is to turn your T-shirt inside out and sew the bottom closed. You will need a sewing machine for this, because you'll need a sturdy. You might not be able to carry a ton of shopping in it, but it would be perfect for togs and towels on the beach, or to hold soft toys.

I found instructions for a **DIY barbecue** on the website of a lady called Dian Thomas in America, which I thought would be great fun to do with children, providing you stand over them at all times! Basically, you take a large tin can, remove the lid and, using a pliers that will cut metal, cut vertical strips of 3cm all the way around – don't cut all the way to the bottom – stop about 6cm from the bottom of the tin. Press the strips into a fan shape, then cover this fan shape with tinfoil. Pop your charcoal in, cover with a little rack and your children will be delighted to grill a few sausages on the beach.

CHAPTER SEVEN

Your Almanac of Household Essentials

<><><><><><><><><><><><><><><><><><><><><><><><><>

*'Cleaning and organising is
a practice, not a project.'*

MEAGAN FRANCIS

When I was young, I used to love reading the *Pears' Cyclopaedia*, a compendium of all kinds of facts and information in one place: everything from historical figures to flags of the world. I used to be fascinated by all the little nuggets of information, and I found out quite recently that it is still going strong. The publishers accurately describe it as 'the Swiss army knife of reference books', which is brilliant! Remembering the cyclopaedia gave me the idea of having a little compendium of my own at the end of this book, full of similar little nuggets, but this time of helpful household information. I hope you'll find it to be useful.

HOME-MADE CLEANERS

HOME RECIPES USING LEMONS

- *As a fridge de-stinker.* Squeeze lemon onto a small piece of cloth or cotton wool and pop it into your fridge door drawer. You can use whole lemons but they go mouldy more quickly in the fridge.

- *To freshen up food.* Of course, a squeeze of lemon juice works wonders in keeping foods like avocado and apple from going brown, but it will also help to freshen a wilted lettuce. Soak your lettuce in the usual way in cold water, but add a few teaspoons of lemon juice to the mix and leave for a little while.

- *As a kitchen cleaner.* Rub your chopping boards with the cut side of a lemon to give them a lovely fresh smell – but be sure that they are clean first! Pour 300ml of warm water into a bowl and squeeze half a lemon in. Drop the rest of the lemon into the bowl and pop into the microwave for a lovely lemony steam clean. Set your microwave for three minutes and keep a close eye on it: more powerful microwaves will cause the water to evaporate more quickly! When the cycle is over, wait a moment before opening the door and removing the bowl. The lemon juice should have loosened all that horrible baked-on food and all you'll need to do is give it a little wipe with a clean wet cloth.

- *As a stain remover on your chopping board or butcher's block.* Simply sprinkle salt onto the stain and scrub with the cut side of half a lemon. Leave to settle overnight and rinse away. Don't use lemons on porous, delicate surfaces, as the acid isn't good for them.

- *As a cleaner for funky lunchboxes.* Rub half a lemon, cut side down, over the lunchbox, then rinse with more lemon juice, leave and then wipe away. At last your lunchbox will smell good!

HOME-MADE MULTIPURPOSE SPRAY

Fill your spray bottle halfway up with water, then to the ¾ way mark with vinegar. To this, add a few drops of an essential oil to mask the vinegar smell (if you don't like it), then add a couple of drops of washing-up liquid. Give it a good shake and you have your very own multi-purpose cleaner.

Not everyone loves the smell of vinegar. If you don't:

- Try adding the peeled rind of a lemon or orange to your spray bottle for some citrus freshness. Leave it for a good while to let the citrus infuse the vinegar.

- Add a few drops of tea-tree oil to your vinegar for a bracing 'clean' smell.

HOME-MADE BEDROOM OR BATHROOM SPRITZ

1 part vodka to 6 parts water, add 10–20 drops of essential oil and spray away the fug.

HOME-MADE CARPET STAIN REMOVER

- 1 part borax substitute
- 1 part baking soda
- 1 part white vinegar

Make into a paste, apply to the stain, let it dry and then vacuum the paste up.

HOME-MADE AIR FRESHENERS

Fill a saucepan three-quarters full with water. Bring to the boil, then turn down to a simmer, add any of the items listed below and enjoy as your kitchen fills with a lovely smell. Keep an eye on your water, though, to avoid it drying out. The great thing about these 'fresheners' is that when it's cold you can keep the mix for a few days.

Add any of the following:

- A sliced orange, a couple of cinnamon sticks and a few cloves.
- A few drops of vanilla extract, some slices of fresh ginger.
- A couple of 'chai' teabags.
- Some almond or coconut extract.
- Sliced limes and a few drops of peppermint oil.

SOME SIMPLE HOME HACKS

FOUR CLEVER WAYS TO CLEAN SPONGES

- Put them in the dishwasher when you have a load on and let all that hot water give them a good clean.

- Use ¾ cup of bleach in ½ litre of water to soak sponges for five minutes. According to *Good Housekeeping*, this is the method that removes the most germs.

- Put your wet-but-not-soaking sponge into the microwave on 'high' for 10–20 seconds – keep an eye on it though!

- Soak your sponge in vinegar overnight. Smelly in a different way, but effective.

KEEPING A BIN FROM LEAKING

Simply pop a bundle of rolled-up newspaper into the bottom of your bin bag to absorb any liquids.

KEEPING WRAPPING PAPER TIDY

Instead of wrapping it with an elastic band, simply cut a cardboard tube from a toilet roll or kitchen roll and insert your wrapping paper.

OPENING A BOTTLE OF WINE – WITHOUT A CORKSCREW!

There are a few ways of doing this, but for God's sake, be careful:

- Push the cork down into the bottle by using an object such as a pen, or a lipstick tube. You can do this by putting your bottle down on a flat surface and by applying downward pressure with your object.

- You can also use a knife in the same way as a corkscrew, pushing it gently into the cork, then working it gently from side to side until it goes all of the way through the cork, then pull. Do this very gently, to avoid accidents.

- You can put the bottle of wine into your shoe – which you have removed from your foot! Then, holding the bottle in one hand, tap your shoe firmly against a wall or tree. Do this a few times and the pressure should push the cork out.

KEEPING YOUR CLOTHES FROM SMELLING IN A LAUNDRY HAMPER OR SUITCASE

Simply add a wrapped bar of soap to the clothes and they'll smell as fresh as can be.

FINDING AN EARRING ON THE CARPET

Place a bit of stocking over the tube of your vacuum cleaner, secure it with a rubber band and, hey presto, when you hoover, you'll see any tiny items.

DESCALING A KETTLE

- Unplug your kettle from the wall – always!
- Fill up to the halfway point with warm water.
- Pour 60ml white vinegar into the water and give it a little swish to mix.
- Leave for half an hour before emptying out the mix and giving the kettle a very gentle wipe with a sponge. Be careful not to damage the heating element!
- Rinse thoroughly with cold water before putting the kettle – with water in it! – on to boil a couple of times to get rid of any vinegar taste.

DRYING WET LEATHER SHOES

There is no quick way of doing this, because all of the quick ways will damage your shoes! You'll need newspapers without dark ink or pictures, which you will ball up into the toe, and continue until your shoe is stuffed with paper. Leave for an hour and come back to check. If the newspaper is soaked, replace it and continue doing so until it stays dry. Leave your shoes to air. This method isn't fast, but it really is the only one that will prevent further leather damage.

HELPING FLOWERS STAY FRESH

One of my nephews used to love *Mythbusters* when he was younger. It was an American show where scientists used to put popular myths to the test using lab techniques. In one test they set up five different vases to compare popular ways of keeping flowers fresh, including vodka, Sprite, apple cider vinegar/sugar, the fridge and an aspirin tablet. They found that Sprite worked fine for a couple of days, but then the sugar affected the flowers – rather like kids after too much lemonade! – and they wilted. They also found that flowers, like humans, can't take too much vodka! So the winner was – the fridge! Before you go to bed at night, pop your flowers into the fridge and they will keep for longer, according to the scientists. And don't forget to use the packet of food that comes with your arrangement too. By the way, the sugar/cider vinegar mix came second. Sugar certainly seems to help flowers, but adding an acid helps to prevent slime. So, there you go!

CLEANING GLASSES

By this, I mean the glasses that you put on your nose! I wear my reading glasses around my neck on a chain, so they are always getting grubby. When I want to clean them, I run them under warm water, then place a drop of washing-up liquid onto each lens. The liquid must be citrus-free, by the way. I rub the liquid in, then rinse with warm water, before giving them a good wipe with a cloth. I can see clearly again!

OPENING JARS

Can there be anything more painful than trying to twist open the lid of a jar? Try these techniques and see if they help:

- Pierce the lid of the jar with a thumb tack – this will break the vacuum inside.

- Tap the bottom of the jar firmly on a flat surface – bubbles will loosen the vacuum seal. You can also tap the lid firmly with a spoon – this has a similar effect.

- Run the lid under hot water for a minute.

- Use something around the lid that will help you to grip it: rubber gloves, a tea towel, a rubber band (handy!) and twist!

RESCUING HOUSE PLANTS WITH YELLOWING LEAVES

If the yellowing is on the tips of the leaves, you need to water more, but if the whole leaf is yellow, you're overdoing it! Make sure your soil is well drained and water when it is barely damp to the touch.

RESCUING COOKING DISASTERS

- *The cake won't come out of the tin.* We've all had this! Try wrapping the still-warm tin in a damp cloth and leaving it. It will loosen the cake.

- *The chocolate has seized.* This means that it's got that gritty texture, a sign that you've gone past the 'glossy' point when melting it, generally because the water in the saucepan over which you're melting the chocolate is boiling, rather than at a very low simmer. If this happens, add a teaspoon or two of milk – I've found that this works. Alternatively, fat will re-emulsify your chocolate: try a teaspoon of melted butter or a teaspoon of olive oil.

- *The egg whites are overbeaten.* Add a fresh egg white to the mix and beat in.

- *The rice is overcooked.* Many people use the steaming method to cook rice, but I've never been able to get the hang of it. The only method that works for me is boiling my rice in plenty of salted water. But what if you overdo it? I find that if I empty the rice into a colander and rinse it thoroughly with cold water, 'fluffing' the rice with a fork as I go, this can rescue me from rice sludge!

- *The spices have been overdone.* It's no wonder that Indian recipes call for yoghurt in sauces – dairy is the best thing for toning down spice, so add a few tablespoons of plain yoghurt to your spicy sauce to give everyone's taste buds a rest.

- *The eggs have curdled.* My mother taught me to add a pinch of flour when I was adding eggs to my sugar and butter mixture to prevent curdling. It works for me! Some people say that this means the finished cake will be rubbery, but I haven't found it to be the case. The simplest thing is to add the eggs very slowly to avoid curdling. And if your cake mix does curdle – don't worry. The final cake will still be fine.

- *Your egg-based sauce has curdled.* This happens when you've overdone the heat. If you act quickly, you can save yourself from having to start again. Try popping the saucepan into ice-cold water to cool it down quickly. If this doesn't work, gently heat some milk (if your sauce is milk-based) or some butter (if butter-based) in a pan, and whisk it into your sauce. You may not be in time to rescue it, but it's worth a try!

- *The sauce is too fatty.* If you have a film of grease on the top of your sauce, simply turn off the heat, let it settle and scoop off the layer of grease that floats to the top. You can even leave your sauce overnight in the fridge before doing this. Another quick fix that I saw – but I haven't tested – is to pop a lettuce leaf onto your sauce – the lettuce draws out the oil, apparently. I'll have to try this next!

- *The bread is stale/rubbery.* Sprinkle it with some water, wrap it in tin foil and pop into a hot oven for a few minutes. The crust should crisp up nicely and the inside will be warm and fresh. I've often done this with baguettes that have gone past their best.

- *The orange/lemon won't peel.* Easy. Pop it into a jug with some boiled water and let stand for a few minutes.

- *You have no eggs.* You're in the middle of a recipe and you open the fridge to get eggs, to find that you don't have any! Half a mashed banana can substitute or, if egg allergy is your issue, 1 tablespoon of ground flaxseeds mixed with 3 tablespoons of warm water. Pureéd apple is also a good egg substitute, but remember, if your recipe calls for a large number of eggs, substitutes won't generally work. If you are using egg substitute in a recipe that you want to rise, try 1 ½ tablespoons of vegetable oil, mixed with the same amount of water and 1 teaspoon of baking powder (not baking soda). This mix will equal one egg in your cake mix.

- *Your boiled egg is leaking.* Add a pinch of salt to the water.

- *You have a ton of strawberries/cherries to stone or hull.* Push a straw through each one – very clever.

KEEPING YOUR HOME SAFE

KITCHEN SAFETY

Any environment that involves using flame, hot liquids and oils and sharp objects should come with a health warning! Of course, many of us take our kitchen environments entirely for granted, but if you have small children, the need for safety becomes particularly important:

- Always, always wash your hands before cooking or eating. If you have long hair, tie it back.

- Store sharp knives safely away from little hands.

- Never leave a boiling saucepan or hot kitchen implement (iron, sandwich maker etc.) unattended.

- Turn your saucepan handles inwards on the stove.

- Buy those little socket blocks so that tiny fingers can't poke into electric sockets.

- Be careful when carrying boiling water to the sink to drain pasta – make sure that there are no children or pets in the way.

- **Your chip pan or fryer need special care.** Do you remember the old ads about chip pan fires? Nowadays, fryers are a great deal safer, but it's still all too easy for a hot pan to catch fire. What can you do if this happens? Pop a lid on the pot, quickly, to put out any sparks or flames. Under no circumstances pour water over the pan – this will make any fire worse. Don't carry the pan outside – you could drop it, or spill more grease in the process. Leave it where it is and smother it with a baking sheet or lid. If you haven't got one, install a smoke alarm – not over the cooker, or it'll go off all the time! – and buy a small fire extinguisher. If in doubt, call 999.

KNIFE SAFETY

The kitchen at The Park has all kinds of handy – and dangerous – machines: blenders, mandolins, sharp knives. All of these require care in handling. The same goes for the domestic kitchen. Don't put your hands near any moving blades (thankfully, blenders are designed not to work without lids) or beaters, and tie your hair back. When working with sharp knives, be sensible. Don't use a great big carving knife to slice carrots! Use the correct knife for the job; use a nice flat surface that won't wobble; don't carry knives with the blade pointing upwards, and when you've finished, don't throw the knife into the sink to soak – so that you cut your hands when you go to wash it. Rinse and clean the knife immediately and put it back into a knife block.

The HSE in the UK has the following list of 'don'ts' to add:

- **Leave knives loose on worktop surfaces where they can be accidentally pushed off.**
- **Try to catch a falling knife.**
- **Use a knife as a can opener.**
- **Carry knives while carrying other objects.**
- **Engage in horseplay with a knife.**
- **Carry a knife in your pocket.**

HOME SAFETY

I like the quote I saw on a greetings card: 'I childproofed my home, but they still get in.' It made me laugh, but it also reminded me about a topic that many of us ignore – whether our homes are safe, particularly if we have young children. I know, we don't feel that our house is a landmine of accidents waiting to happen, but the truth is, the home is a common place for accidents, and accidents are the commonest cause of death for toddlers, and account for half of all deaths among 10–15-year-olds. Sobering statistics.

- Every home should have a smoke alarm, a carbon monoxide alarm and a fire extinguisher. Check them regularly to make sure that the batteries are fresh. Most devices will start to beep when the battery is getting low, but if in doubt, check your device regularly: add it to your monthly cleaning schedule or put a reminder in your phone so you can't forget. I have found that it's very, very easy for your grill or frying pan to catch fire – all you need is a few drops of fat to spatter into the flame and, before you know it, fire is shooting up into the cooker hood. It's happened to me!

- Never, ever put water on cooker flames; instead, quickly turn off the heat source and smother the flames with the lid of your pot, if you can. If the fire has gone out, take the pot out into the garden and leave it on a non-flammable surface to cool down. If the fire is bigger or you can't put it out, use your fire blanket or fire extinguisher. Always keep one of these handy: you can buy small ones at hardware stores.

- Make sure that everyone in the house knows how to get out in the event of a fire. Nowadays, we often lock windows when we go out for security reasons. Make sure that you know where your window keys are in case of an emergency.

- Close all doors that lead on to your hallway, which may be the best escape route for you in case of a fire.

- Switch off all appliances when you are going to bed; this applies particularly to dishwashers, which should have finished their cycle when you go off to bed. I remember that my sister Kate set her dishwasher to run while they went off for the day on a Bank Holiday Monday. They came back at teatime and Kate's son noticed smoke swirling in the living room. Peter warned them not to open the door, and broke a tiny 'fly' window, inserting a hose to cool the room down. The fireman told them that dishwashers are the source of a disproportionate number of home accidents.

- Make sure that your clothes dryer lint tray is emptied regularly – lint is a fire hazard and can build up quickly.

- Check that any fuel-burning appliances are serviced and maintained, as they can leak carbon monoxide. It is odourless, meaning you won't be aware of it – so it's all the more important to install a carbon monoxide alarm. Did you know that any fuel can release carbon monoxide, be it coal, oil, wood or gas. So don't let any air vents get blocked, or indeed, put anything in front of air vents, and check that flues and chimneys are clear.

- Practise a fire drill at home to make sure that everyone knows what to do in case of a fire and knows the quickest – and safest – route to safety. Impress upon your family that no one should ever go into a house that's on fire.

According to the HSE, the most dangerous areas are the kitchen, bathroom and stairs, and the most common hazards are choking, suffocating, falling, burning/scalding and drowning. I know this might sound very depressing, but it shows that it really pays to be aware of home safety, particularly with the two most vulnerable groups: small children and older people.

If you want to keep your child safe:

- Don't put pillows or throws into a baby's cot, and make sure that they can't slip down into any sleeping bags.

- Keep plastic bags safely out of children's reach.

- Make sure that things like buttons are well sewn onto garments and upholstery, as children can choke on them.

- Keep all hot items like saucepans, irons and anything involving hot water well out of reach. My friend Cathy tells me that she trained herself to put pots and pans only on the back burners of the stove when the children were small, and to turn pot handles inwards. And don't forget your taps – you can set your hot water thermostat to go no higher than a safe temperature: if you can't work out how to do this yourself, ask a plumber.

- Keep all of your household cleaners in a high cupboard, with one of those childproof catches on it. Brightly coloured bottles look tempting to small children.

- The same goes for pills and medicines. Thank God for those childproof lids on bottles nowadays, but it still pays to keep everything in a locked box or cabinet, well out of reach.

- Keep all flexes up high, away from curious hands, as children might pull something down on top of themselves.

- Always put a fireguard on any open fires or 'indeed' around any wood-burning stoves or ranges. Place a safety gate at the top and bottom of the stairs, but also in front of the kitchen: if you have to leave to go and answer the telephone, you can pop your little one at the other side and rest assured that they won't be able to wander into the kitchen.

- Tuck any blind cords neatly away from any wandering hands and be careful about cots placed near to blinds – make sure that no cord is dangling.

- Secure all furniture to the wall or floor, so that children can't pull anything down on top of themselves.

- It really does pay to make sure that your child's clothing fits well and doesn't have fringing or other items hanging off it that might catch on anything or, indeed, catch fire. Be particularly mindful of fancy dress costumes, which are often made in synthetic fabrics and often have fringing or capes, both fire hazards, particularly at Halloween.

- Bath time should be a pleasure for your little ones, and you should supervise them at all times, as you should with paddling pools or garden ponds. I have a friend whose child was fascinated by the pond in his granny's garden and used to spend a lot of time hovering over it, throwing little pebbles in. Sensibly, Granny had a mesh guard fitted into the pond to avoid any accidents. Domestic swimming pools should always be fenced in, for safety's sake.

- Make sure that any equipment you buy is safe for your children. Use a harness to keep them from climbing out of their high chair and examine any equipment for sharp edges. Make sure that any 'vintage' toys or beds are safe. Granny might want you to use the cot you had as a child for your baby, but it will definitely not meet today's safety standards! Decline, even if you fear hurting her feelings – your child's safety is paramount.

YOUR HOME FIRST-AID KIT

Every home should have one! You'll find little first-aid kits in many hardware and car stores and even the supermarket, so keep an eye out for them. I think one in the car and one at home is the ideal: you don't want to find yourself without it if someone has taken the car! I looked into the contents of the commercial first-aid kits and found that they generally contain the following:

- A range of plasters in different sizes.
- Some gauze for wrapping around burns or wounds and some tape to seal the gauze.
- Some burn gel pads for minor burns.
- An antiseptic cream and wipes.
- A tweezers and some safety pins.
- Insect bite spray.
- An eye-wash cup.
- Sunscreen.

To your home kit, you could also add:

- Pain relief tablets – ibuprofen and paracetamol.

- An antihistamine.

- Something for tummy upsets.

- Antibacterial hand gel.

- A thermometer.

- A couple of pairs of disposable gloves.

- Hydrocortisone cream – for insect bites and other rashes.

- A first-aid manual. There's no point in having an elaborate kit if you don't know how to use it. Even better, do a one-day first-aid course, so that you are well versed in the basics, should the worst happen.

- A little torch is a great addition to a first-aid kit – make it one of those handy wind-up ones, so that you don't have to find batteries in the dead of night.

EPILOGUE

Epilogue

*'When it comes to housework the one
thing no book of household management
can ever tell you is how to begin. Or
maybe I mean why.'*

KATHERINE WHITEHORN

I have enjoyed every minute of researching and writing this book, from finding out about ancient housekeeping lore to updating my knowledge of recycling and cleaning difficult fabrics. I've picked up quite a lot of really useful information and now feel ready to tackle household tasks that I'm avoiding, particularly when it comes to tidying! We all have our weak spots and, I have to confess, clutter is mine.

Writing this book has also helped me to recall and share happy memories of my home life in Ballaly and in County Sligo, and, of course, the many near misses and quick fixes that come with being in the hotel business. I hope you have enjoyed these too, and will have picked up some handy hints along the way. If there's one thing I myself have taken away from this book, it's that 'little and often' is the key!

More importantly though, I've come to understand that life has come a long way since the time of Mrs Beeton, who declared: 'Among the gifts that nature has bestowed on women, few rank higher than the capacity for domestic management, for the exercise of this faculty constantly affects the happiness, comfort and prosperity of the whole family.'

Nowadays, nature bestows the gift of domestic management on mums, dads, kids and everyone who lives in a shared home. It's no longer just about Mum looking after everyone. That is my 'philosophy', if you like, and it's one I hope you will have taken with you after reading this little book: that looking after a home is everyone's responsibility.

I have spent most of my adult life looking after people, and it's something that gives me a great deal of pleasure. It doesn't matter where our guests come from, or even how they behave: what's important to me is that they are happy and comfortable at our hotel. I also know that our guests' happiness depends on the hard work of all of the people who help us at the hotel, who get up every morning at the crack of dawn to begin the tasks of the day, and who are there late at night, long after the last guest has gone to bed.

For me, this is what housekeeping is really about: not a tedious list of chores that 'have to be done', hanging over us like the sword of Damocles!

It's about making a home comfortable for everyone who lives there, and because we live in the 21st century, this is now a shared task, with everyone pitching in. Working as a team means that there will be inevitable mishaps, burnt shirts and flooded ceilings, but it also means that we are all in it together, sharing the burden and making life a bit easier for each other. What could be better than that.